Upper Cumberland
Country

The Cumberland River winding through southern Cumberland County, Kentucky
(Photo by the author)

William Lynwood Montell, General Editor

FOLKLIFE IN THE SOUTH SERIES

Upper Cumberland Country

William Lynwood Montell

WITH A FOREWORD BY *Mary Robbins*

University Press of Mississippi   Jackson

Library of Congress Cataloging-in-Publication Data

Montell, William Lynwood, 1931–
    Upper Cumberland country / William Lynwood
Montell ; with a foreword by Mary Robbins.
        p.   cm. — (Folklife in the South series)
    Includes bibliographical references and index.
    ISBN 0-87805-630-0. — ISBN 0-87805-631-9 (pbk.)
    1. Cumberland River Valley (Ky. and Tenn.)—
Social life and customs.   2. Folklore—Cumberland
River Valley (Ky. and Tenn.)   I. Title.   II. Series.
F442.2.M664   1993
976.8'5—dc20   93-6972
                                                CIP

British Library Cataloging-in-Publication data available

Dedicated with deepest appreciation

TO MY PARENTS
Willie and Hazel Montell

TO MY CHILDREN
Monisa and Brad

AND TO MY GRANDSONS
Alex, Frank, Hunter, Robert, and Tyler,
from whom much is expected in keeping family traditions alive

C o n t e n t s

For over three decades, Dr. William Lynwood Montell, carrying his ever-present camera and tape recorder, has been a familiar and much-loved figure in the hills and valleys of the Upper Cumberland region of Kentucky and Tennessee. In 1982, when I first met him, he had already carved out an impressive niche for himself in the fields of folklore and oral history. In so doing, Montell had earned the respect and admiration of his peers as well as of the individuals whose lives and times he had chronicled in his journeys across what we here in north central Tennessee call "God's country."

My introduction to Dr. Montell, or Lyn as I have come to know him, was the result of the suggestion of a mutual friend on the faculty of Tennessee Technical University, who recommended him as a guest for "Tennessee Writers," a program that I produced and hosted for the Cookeville PBS television station. I will always remember my total absorption and absolute delight in *Ghosts Along the Cumberland: Deathlore in the Kentucky Foothills*, the first of Lyn's books that I read in preparation for the television interview.

That reading made me cognizant of the richness of my own heritage. Growing up in the Upper Cumberland, I had been aware, as had most young people of my generation, of the region's history and folklore but in a very superficial way. The stories that my older relatives told belonged to another era and another way of life, one that had little or no meaning in today's "modern" world.

Lynwood Montell's writing changed completely and forever my concepts of time and place and my ideas regarding the continuity of family. After I finished *Ghosts Along the Cumberland*, I quickly read everything that he had written. I also became involved in several of his oral history projects, as well as initiating some of my own.

The pages that follow contain some of the most significant material that he has collected and documented. In spanning several generations and many diverse aspects of life in the region, Montell has successfully conveyed the continuity of heritage. For everyone who believes as I do that it is important to capture and preserve the folkways of the present as well as the past, this book will be a treasure. For others, it will be a fascinating "read" and no doubt will make believers of them also.

This book is my story, the story of my family and neighbors, and the story of all the people who have ever lived in the Upper Cumberland, past and present. It is also Lynwood Montell's story, for this chronicle is written with love and respect for a place and a people who are his own. It is told with the flair of the master storyteller and the skill and integrity of the true folklorist and oral historian.

To Dr. William Lynwood Montell, who continues to dedicate his life to the preservation of our heritage, I extend my gratitude. To Lyn Montell, my good friend and respected coworker on many projects over the past several years, I reaffirm my admiration and respect. May he continue to seek and find the treasures that lie just around the bend of every winding road in the Upper Cumberland.

To the reader, whether your roots are in the region or not, may you find a bit of yourself on the pages that follow. Those who do will be most fortunate.

Mary Robbins
Travel Development Coordinator
Upper Cumberland Development District
Cookeville, Tennessee

Acknowledgments

While I did some recent field and archival research in preparation for writing this book, much of the data presented here derives from years of fieldwork conducted in connection with previous writing projects. When I began to organize and write the present volume in 1990, I was constantly reminded of the many people who had assisted me in my efforts to gather material.

First of all I wish to acknowledge my debt to the narrators/interviewees who shared with me their priceless treasure of firsthand and traditional knowledge. These custodians of regional heritage are identified by name, either in chapter context or in the bibliographical notes. Without their contributions, there would be no book on Upper Cumberland folklife.

A number of other individuals were indispensable in various ways to the successful completion of this book. Especially helpful as archival, library, and field researchers, and as readers of the manuscript in its various stages of completion, were folklorist and education curator Dianne Watkins of Western Kentucky University's Kentucky Museum; Rebecca Hornal, folk studies undergraduate student, and Joseph Ruff, folk studies graduate student. Other graduate students at Western Kentucky University, including Trudy Balcom, Susan Johnstad, Janice Molloy, John Morgan, Melinda Pennington, and Janice Phillips, also contributed insights that appear throughout the book.

Others who assisted in different ways include Sam and Katherine Anderson and Bob Dudney, Gainesboro; Ed Brooks, Calvin Dickinson, Homer Kemp, Judy Roberson, Mary Robbins, and Larry Whittaker, all of Cookeville; David Cross and Sue Williams, Albany; Dr. Joe Nunley, Murfreesboro; Judy Hetrick, Indiana University; Gerald Gernt and Ed Wiley, Jamestown, Tennessee; and Fern Roe, Carthage.

I am grateful to a number of librarians and archivists, especially Patricia Hodges and Sue Lynn McGuire in Western Kentucky University's Kentucky Library, Bowling Green; Fran Schell, director of the Tennessee State Library and Archives, Nashville; Linda Anderson, Kentucky Historical Society Library, Frankfort; and staff in the Pickett County Library, Byrdstown; and the Cookeville Public Library.

I wish also to thank Karen Kallstrom, departmental secretary for the Department of Modern Languages and Intercultural Studies at Western Kentucky University, who helped me in numerous ways, and Brunessa Beckles, Alice Ann Bivin, and Allison Whitley, student assistants who transcribed numerous field-recorded tapes and provided other invaluable services.

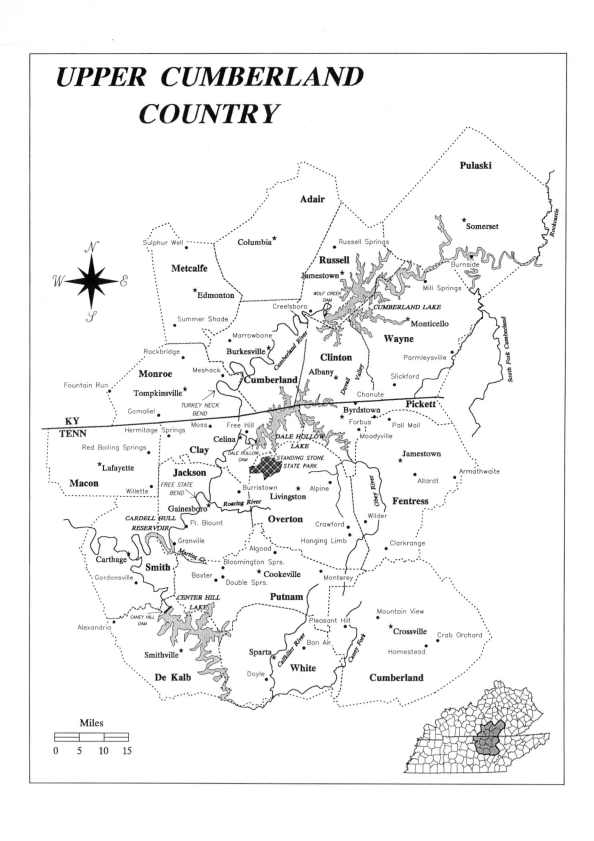

UPPER CUMBERLAND COUNTRY

Miles

0   5   10   15

Americans have been aware of distinct regions in this country since colonial times. Delegates at the Continental Congress in 1774 used the designations *Southern, Middle, Eastern,* and *New England.* By the time the United States was settled at the end of the nineteenth century, a host of new regions could be named, including the Midwest, Great Plains, Southwest, West, Intermountain Basin, and Pacific Northwest.

It is common to hear such terms as *district, division, territory,* and *section* used by state and federal planners to identify clusters of states and counties. However, the terms *region* and *subregion* are still much in vogue these days when people wish to identify a physical place. If the identification is personal, it can evoke fond memories and emotional responses to home and to the land itself. Lewis Wirth comments on such matters in *Regionalism in America,* defining regionalism as a state of mind, a way of life, and a mode of collective thought. These features—according to Wirth, produce a settled way of life, a characteristic consciousness, a sense of mutual interdependence, and a feeling of common belonging and sharing—are associated with heritage and folklife in an area such as the Upper Cumberland of Kentucky and Tennessee, the subregion described in this book.

The study of folklife is the study of vernacular regional culture, that is, what people do on an everyday basis. Don Yoder, father of folklife investigation in the United States, writes that "folk culture is traditional culture, bound by tradition and transmitted by tradition, and is (although not exclusively) rural and pre-industrial." Studies in the everyday aspects of human life and thought rely on oral recollections, both personal and collective; published descriptions of daily life; and observations, photographs, and cogent descriptions of informal, tradition-oriented contemporary activities that are performed on a regular basis by individuals and groups within the region.

The term *folk* is used to identify those persons, past and present, who pass along beliefs, customs, practices, songs, stories, and ways of life, largely unconsciously, from one generation to the next without the aid of formal educational processes, producing a traditional culture that arises organically and dictates the character of local and regional life styles.

Traditions, both old and new, are also communicated from person to person and group to group within the same generation. Folklore, as such traditions are called, exists only through performance, taking place on an individual basis when traditional knowledge provides the groundwork of thought and action, and also when people come together to interact with each other. In this connection it should be pointed out that folklore typically knows no racial, gender, or social boundaries. Folklife is a broader term that refers to the composite of all the folkloristic ways of thought and action known and practiced by individuals, families, and other groups within a region.

This book provides a description of the dominant folk cultural forms and activities, then and now, relevant to the Upper Cumberland area in Kentucky and Tennessee. Much of this region's folklife springs from the frontier period that began at the end of the eighteenth century and has continued through the years because of generational occupation of the same soil, decades of shared experiences, and a strong desire to maintain cultural stability. In *American Folklore*, Richard M. Dorson defined a folk region as a place where the "people are wedded to the land, and the land holds memories."

More recent forms of regional folklife, however voguish they appear, typically derive from earlier modes of life, thought, and action. Teen cruising is a case in point. Those who participate in cruising and hanging out wear the newest fads in clothing and drive cars and trucks acceptable to their peers. Yet their parents and grandparents also engaged in forms of socializing in horse-drawn vehicles and automobiles—behavior that was often viewed as nonconformist by members of the older generations at that time.

As described in this book, the Upper Cumberland subregion is a bistate entity comprising all or portions of Adair (Columbia is the county seat), Clinton (Albany), Cumberland (Burkesville), Metcalfe (Edmonton), Monroe (Tompkinsville), Pulaski (Somerset), Russell (Jamestown), and Wayne (Monticello) counties in south central Kentucky, and Clay (Celina), Cumberland (Crossville), DeKalb (Smithville), Fentress (Jamestown), Jackson (Gainesboro), Macon (Lafayette), Overton (Livingston), Pickett (Byrdstown), Putnam (Cookeville), Smith (Carthage), and White (Sparta) counties in central and north central Tennessee. All Tennessee counties listed here are members of the federally defined Upper Cumberland Development District, Cookeville, which includes an additional five counties. With the exception of Metcalfe and Monroe, the Kentucky counties are affiliated with the Lake Cumberland Area Development District, Russell Springs.

In *The Upper Cumberlands*, Willis B. Boyd described the region in these glowing terms:

The Upper Cumberland District, located at the very heart and center of eastern America, is high enough and far enough north to escape the enervating effects of the Deep South, and far enough south to enjoy long summers with short mild winters. The hills are high enough to be cool but not high enough to be cold; the valleys are low enough to be warm but not low enough to be hot.

The Upper Cumberland is not *southern* in its folkways, nor is it *Appalachian*. People here never had grits for breakfast until this southern dish was introduced by fast-food chain restaurants. And while residents of the Upper Cumberland may be somewhat more closely aligned to Appalachia than they are to the Deep South, they do not view themselves as a part of Southern Appalachia. Upper Cumberlanders typically picture their Appalachian neighbors to the east in stereotypical terms, i. e., as mountaineers, people who have a distinct speech pattern, and poor souls who were bypassed by modern times. On the other hand, occupants of the Upper Cumberland recognize themselves to be the epitome of America's hillbillies and may even use the term in referring to themselves. Many fights have ensued, however, when that term, along with the equally derogative "briar," has been cast at them by outsiders in northern and midwestern urban centers.

The Upper Cumberland is a distinctive entity not only in terms of its folk culture but in its geographical location as well. If one were to place a hypothetical clock in the center of the region (roughly northern Overton County), then use the numerals on the dial (with twelve o'clock pointing northward) as the means of locating the region in relation to other geographical zones, the Appalachian area would extend from one to five; southern Tennessee from five to seven; the Nashville Basin from seven to nine; Tennessee's Highland Rim from nine to ten; the Barrens and the Knobs of Kentucky from ten to twelve; and the Outer Bluegrass from twelve to one.

The Cumberland River, now blocked by two flood control dams, was the main waterway in the region. It served as the principal means of travel and freight transport for residents during most of the nineteenth century and, for most of the counties traversed by the river itself, the first three decades of the twentieth century. This historic stream heads in the mountains of eastern Kentucky, then flows in a westerly course by way of Pineville and Williamsburg before dropping over a high ledge to form the Cumberland Falls sixty-eight nautical miles above Burnside. From Burnside, once important as the head of navigation on the river, the Cumberland flows in magnificent bends as it continues its westerly journey across southern Kentucky. At Turkey Neck Bend in eastern Monroe County, it takes a rather sudden turn to the south and empties into Tennessee just above Celina. Subsequently washing the outskirts of Gainesboro, Granville, and Carthage, at Nashville the river gently turns northwestward en route back across Kentucky for a rendezvous with the Ohio River at Smithland.

Smaller rivers that drain the region and helped to shape area folklife include the Caney Fork, which flows across White, DeKalb, and Smith counties before joining the Cumberland at Carthage; the Obey, a tributary stream that receives the thundering waters of the Wolf River and, with it, drains much of the rugged portions of Clay, Overton, Fentress, and Pickett before emptying into the Cumberland at Celina; and the Roaring River, a rivulet that cuts through the beautiful hill country of Overton and Jackson counties on its way to the Cumberland just north of Gainesboro.

The Upper Cumberland is a region physically characterized by lush river and creek valleys, secluded coves, and upland areas that range from beautifully sculptured rolling hills and plateaus to low-mountain terrain. The two most prominent features are the Cumberland River Valley, stretching southward from Burnside to Carthage, and the Cumberland Plateau, an escarpment-faced, stream-carved surface some two thousand feet above sea level, which extends north to south across portions of Fentress, Cumberland, Overton, Putnam, White, and Van Buren counties. The valley and plateau are both characterized by a mild, four-season climate.

While Cookeville and Somerset have grown into regional urban centers in recent times, the Upper Cumberland is still by and large a rural bastion. Although most people in the area now work in the county seat towns in factories, banks, hospitals, hardware and department stores, and produce houses, many of them continue to live in rural areas on ancestral lands as did their parents and grandparents before them. This familiarity with the land provides pleasant memories and a strong sense of generational continuity.

Many residents of the area continue to till the soil, although their equipment reflects the influence of modern technology and concomitant capital investments. Some people who do not till the soil on a regular basis still raise livestock or allow a corporate farmer to do it for them. Cattle of varying sizes, varieties, and colors dot the landscape during all seasons of the year, creating scenes of pastoral loveliness as they graze on the green hillsides or lie in the fields, basking in the warm rays of the sun.

The Upper Cumberland is also home to city and town dwellers whose roots are as deep there as those of their rural neighbors. They too have fond recollections of growing up in the region, of playing in groups on

empty city lots, of attending scouting camps each season, and of trying to keep their sweethearts from paying too much attention to "those country kids."

Finally, there are people in rural and urban areas alike who have annual monetary incomes well below the poverty level. But those who live in the Upper Cumberland share certain traditions and values that provide a feeling of coherence within the region. Heritage is a precious resource, and that is what folklife is all about.

Research for this book on Upper Cumberland folklife actually began in 1959 when D. K. Wilgus, then my mentor, and I made numerous forays into the Cumberland River country (sometimes accompanied by country music authority Archie Green) to track down historical legends and songs about such local characters as Joe Coleman, who was hanged in Burkesville in 1846 on the charge of killing his wife with a butcher knife; the Civil War renegade guerrilla, Beanie Short, known across Clay,

Family farms still exist, though in declining numbers. Here a young motorcyclist rounds up cattle for the evening milking session, 1992. (Photo by the author)

Cumberland, and Monroe Counties for his nefarious activities and his death at the hands of Union bushwackers; and Clure and Joe Williams, two Cumberland River logging/rafting brothers from Celina celebrated in story and song for allegedly killing a steamboat captain in the 1890s. Wilgus and I interviewed and tape-recorded numerous old-time musicians, and sometimes folk medical practitioners as well.

As a folklore graduate student at Indiana University from 1960 to 1963, I actively tape-recorded blacks and whites alike in my quest for information about the Coe Ridge community of black freedmen in southern Cumberland County, Kentucky. The information gathered in that connection was used for my doctoral dissertation and then in my first book, *The Saga of Coe Ridge: A Study in Oral History*, published in 1970. The data compiled during those interviews reached far beyond the history of blacks in the area, including much else about regional folklife. I have drawn upon portions of this material in putting together the present volume.

The years from 1975 to 1985 were particularly important ones in terms of obtaining photographs, tape recordings and other information relevant to Upper Cumberland folklife. Three additional books resulted from that decade of fieldwork—fieldwork that indirectly provided a tremendous base of information about the region's people and their folklife forms.

I have devoted one-third of a century to the study of various aspects of Upper Cumberland history, life, and culture. Obviously, change has come to the region during that period of time; I have attempted to observe and record these changes and to understand why they took place. While physical differences are apparent everywhere, the element of tradition was and still is important in the lives of the people who live there. This book attempts to explore the role of tradition in shaping the region's folklife.

The subject matter in the present volume is grouped into three sections. Part one comprises a historical overview of the Upper Cumberland and its people, from the Native Americans who first occupied the area to the ethnic and religious groups that have arrived within recent times. Part two describes the economic self-sufficiency of the early generations, then focuses attention on their beliefs, customs, practices, and other forms of folklore pertaining to education, religion, medicine, and death. Part three is an examination of contemporary pre-teen and teen culture and of adult social and gender-bonding activities. While many facets of regional folklore and folklife are dealt with in this volume, the central point of concern is what people do when they get together informally.

The present study rests on the assumption that before American life and culture can be fully understood, cogent descriptions of regional folklife must be written. If this book, along with other titles in the Folklife in the South series, leads to serious reader interest in these matters, it will have served its purpose.

Historical
Perspectives

A Rich Legacy

In 1748 an adventurous group of Virginia gentry under the leadership of Dr. Thomas Walker rode through a gap in the mountains in the southwestern corner of their state to discover what lay beyond. Walker and his men gave the name Cumberland, for the Duke of Cumberland, to the mountains, the gap, and the river that originated nearby. They followed the Cumberland River as it twisted and turned in great bends on its westerly course through southern Kentucky before disappearing into Tennessee just above present-day Celina. From there the river meandered through the Nashville Basin and then back across Kentucky, where it joined the Ohio River at Smithland.

Later explorers gave the name Upper Cumberland to the Tennessee area between the Cumberland Plateau on the east and the Cumberland River on the west. Then in the late 1820s, steamboat personnel reiterated the name Upper Cumberland when they assigned it to that portion of the river and its hinterland between Carthage, Tennessee, and Burnside, Kentucky (the head of navigation). Area institutions, associations, and businesses since that time have frequently used the term, and many still do.

Throughout the 1760s and early 1770s, groups called Long Hunters (so named because their expeditions lasted for weeks or months, even infrequently as long as two years) from Virginia and North Carolina made forays into the Upper Cumberland area, covering virtually every inch of it in the process. The most famous of the Long Hunters was Daniel Boone, but different ones gave their names to creeks, rivers, knobs, and other landmarks. Their visits greatly disturbed the Native Americans who, long before, had laid claim to the area as permanent tribal hunting grounds.

NATIVE AMERICAN OCCUPANCY

The Upper Cumberland was long the domain of prehistoric cave dwellers, who subsisted by hunting and fishing, and some agricultural tribes, who made fine pottery and lived in large fortified towns. From stone, wood, shell, and bone, these first occupants of the Upper

Cumberland created the containers and implements necessary for home use as well as items needed in hunting and fishing activities. Beautifully ornamented pottery, wooden bowls, and spoons made from shells have been recovered from various prehistoric sites. Those who fished fashioned for themselves basketry traps, weirs, nets, spears, bone hooks, and projectile points. Hunters had easy access to bows, arrows, and reed-guns. Stone axes and knives served as warrior weapons.

These early occupants were likely the ancestors of the Cherokees, Creeks, Chickamaugas, Chickasaws, Iroquois, and Shawnees. It is generally said that neither of the latter groups dared live in the region for fear of attack from the others who claimed it as their hunting ground. To help alleviate the problem, the Chickasaws and Cherokees established a boundary line dividing their lands at a gigantic stone near present-day Monterey in Putnam County.

Trails across the Upper Cumberland forged by bison and deer were used by Native American tribes in the area and by later-arriving white settlers. On the Tennessee side, three major trails criss-crossed the region. The Chickamauga Path began at the Indian settlements in north Georgia, entering the Upper Cumberland at the southern tip of Warren County. Continuing northward, the path forked at the site of the ancient fortified Indian village at Cherry Hill in north central White County. The eastern fork intersected Tollunteeskee's Trail in Cumberland County, then continued northward to the East-West Trail near present-day Jamestown. Tollunteeskee's Trail itself came out of east Tennessee and passed westward across the Upper Cumberland by way of Cumberland, Overton, Jackson, and Smith counties on its way to what is now Nashville. Portions of this latter historic trail took on several other names as white settlers entered the Upper Cumberland. These included the North Carolina Military Road, Avery's Trace, Cumberland Trace, Old North Carolina Trace, and the Walton Road. The last of the four Indian arteries is the Great East-West Trail that passed in a northwesterly direction across what are now Fentress and Pickett counties before entering the southeastern corner of present-day Clinton County, Kentucky.

The East-West Trail continued in a westerly course across Clinton and Cumberland counties, crossing into what is now Monroe County near the Center Point community. From there the trail followed a buffalo trace that traversed the hilly terrain in a southeast-northwest direction pointing toward Metcalfe County. Area residents still refer to this historic communications link as The Old Trace Road.

Numerous stories about the first occupants of the Upper Cumberland are still told by the descendants of the pioneers who displaced them. A few of these narratives describe hostile confrontations between the two races and call certain Indian chieftains by name. Chief Obeds reputedly headed up the Nettle Carrier Indians, a small band of Cherokee farmers-potters-basket makers. This legendary group of stragglers remained undetected for some years near Alpine in Overton County. Tradition holds that Chief Obeds lived in this portion of the Upper Cumberland until 1799 and then departed for East Tennessee. His tribe chose to remain behind and were eventually absorbed into the local white culture that surrounded them on all sides.

Numerous legends still told across the region claim that small bands of friendly warriors returned to the area for decades after the departure of their ancestors. Invariably they were searching for tribal treasures that had been left behind when their people had to make a hasty retreat. Whites and blacks alike tell these stories. It is not unusual for people in the region today to boast of an ancestor—three, four, or five generations removed—who was "full-blooded Cherokee Indian."

THE COMING OF THE PIONEERS

Anglo settlement of the Upper Cumberland followed closely on the heels of the Revolutionary War. Even then, efforts at colonization proved difficult in most instances because of understandable Indian hostility and resistance. By the 1790s, however, with the establishment of Fort Blount on the Cumberland River south of present-day Gainesboro, most of the Indians in Tennessee were removed either by treaty or warfare or both.

The earliest settlements in the entire Upper Cumberland began in Kentucky at Parmleysville in 1780, according to Harriette Arnow. It was Cherokee country then; today it is Wayne County. That same year, Hugh Roberts, a Pennsylvania Quaker who migrated to what is now Clay County, Tennessee, to avoid military service, settled near the mouth of the Obey River. Two years later, William Dale located on the Obey just above the Roberts place. Two additional settlements were established in Tennessee's Upper Cumberland in 1786. These were at Lilydale, located at the junction of the Wolf and Obey rivers on the East-West Trail in Clay County, and Fort Blount, strategically situated on the Cumberland River in present-day Jackson County near Flynn's Lick. In late 1789, Cumberland, Metcalfe, and Monroe counties in Kentucky witnessed the arrival of a handful of families at or near present-day Burkesville, Edmonton, and Tompkinsville.

In 1791, a district was set aside for the Cherokees, the western boundary of which extended in a southwesterly direction from the Big South Fork River (a tributary of the Cumberland) in Kentucky to a line separating the Cumberland and Duck rivers forty-five miles above

Nashville. This line divided Tennessee's Upper Cumberland into two equal parts. The area located west of the line was open for settlement; the mountainous area to the east was reserved for the Cherokees, except that whites could now pass through the territory "free and unmolested." By 1797 more than a dozen new Tennessee settlements had been established.

With the signing of the Third Treaty of Tellico in 1805, most of Tennessee's remaining Upper Cumberland was purchased from the Cherokees. Additional white settlements soon dotted the countryside. Because of mountain-like terrain and inaccessible escarpments, settlers entered the southern portions of Tennessee's Upper Cumberland by going to the Nashville Basin and then making an approach from the west.

The first white settlers in the Upper Cumberland mainly came from Virginia and the Carolinas, although Pennsylvania provided quite a few of the newcomers. Primarily of Irish, English, and German extraction, they took up homesteads, opening small clearings on the land where they built log cabins and houses that would suffice to shelter their families during the settlement phase and lend credibility to their dreams of permanence.

Most of these pioneers brought along functional items such as iron kettles, feather beds, quilts, seed for the first year's planting, and the necessary farming implements and tools. They also brought traditional ideas about farming, tending livestock, hunting and fishing, preparing food, schooling of the young, socializing, and worshipping God. Many of these traditions would undergo change, however, in the demanding new environment. If they had been accustomed to frequent and formal worship, they soon learned, in the words of Overton County resident George A. Knight, "to get along with visits from circuit riders, brush-arbor meetings, and services held under the shade of spreading oak trees."

The early agriculture of the white settlers was subsistence in nature. Corn, the major crop of the Native American tribes, became the mainstay of Anglo farming as well. Easy to plant in the newly cleared ground between stumps and dead trees, corn grew well in this fertile environment and provided bountiful harvests for that day and time, especially during the second year after tree roots and stumps had rotted or been chopped away. Other than hay, corn was about the only crop grown by the early settlers. Since parent settlements were hundreds of miles away in Virginia, North Carolina, or Pennsylvania, and there were no established roads leading back to them over the mountain-like terrain, corn provided the newcomers with economic independence, supplying an abundance of food for humans and animals alike. Wheat, rye, oats, barley, hemp, and flax soon supplemented these initial crops, as Upper

Cumberland farm families demonstrated that they were firmly situated and there to stay.

The river bottomlands afforded fertile soil, but most early families chose to live in the uplands, where the land was rich with humus that had accumulated over the centuries. It was generally felt that the river bottoms were unhealthy areas, where typhoid and malaria might be found. Too, experience soon revealed that floods posed constant threats to lives and crops. Some families who had first settled in the creek and river bottoms abandoned their homes and rebuilt higher up on the adjacent slopes and benches. Yet those who chose to remain behind, while frequently experiencing the ravages of nature in the spring, were in the long run more prosperous financially and culturally than their neighbors who had moved to higher ground.

Clearing the land of trees to make room for agricultural pursuits was a task faced by pioneers and subsequent generations until the early years of the twentieth century. Residents approached this major hurdle com-

A Macon County farmer in the early 1970s, tilling the land much as his pioneer forbears did (Photo by the author)

munally, as a dozen or so men would unite efforts in cutting the trees, trimming away the tops and limbs and stacking the brush into piles, rolling the huge logs together, and burning them after adequate drying had taken place. In the words of James Hiram Smith, native of Russell County, "When you were clearing off a newground, everything was set up to be burned."

The sizes of farms in the Upper Cumberland varied depending on terrain. Small acreages were the rule in the low hill-narrow valley areas, while prominent creek and river bottoms fostered larger land holdings that were often tilled by black people who had been brought in as slaves. Whatever the situation regarding the sizes and locales of area farms and the nature of the labor force, the Upper Cumberland moved rather quickly from frontier times to the farming era. By the time of the Civil War, the agrarian way of life was firmly instituted. However, the four years of strife from 1861 to 1865 during the war virtually wiped out the region's commercial farming enterprises, and the financial loss was even greater for the few large landholders whose slaves were freed.

During Reconstruction, the system of farm tenancy or sharecropping was introduced. But the larger landholders, now forced to borrow money to continue operations, often found themselves unable to meet mortgage payments. Some of them became tenants on the farms that were once theirs.

The average annual cash income was minimal during those trying post-war years. A resident of the Slickford community of Wayne County during that era owned two hundred acres of land, yet was hard-pressed each year to come up with the sixty cents necessary to pay property taxes. Former members of the landed-gentry class were no better off after the war than their upland neighbors, as neither class was able to accumulate a surplus of cash.

Beginning around 1890, some of the ex-slaves, along with members of the first black generation born during the post–Civil War years, left the region for what promised to be a better life in midwestern urban areas such as Indianapolis, Chicago, and Kansas City. About that same time, a few area whites went to Kansas each fall to work as wheat harvesters, following the machines northward until they reached the Dakotas. Others went to Indiana and Illinois to work in the corn harvests, doing so through the Great Depression that gripped the entire country in the 1930s. These harvest-time activities provided men with a little extra cash to help their families get through the winter months ahead.

Farm income and farm wages in the Upper Cumberland were especially deplorable for whites and blacks alike during the first three decades of the twentieth century. William H. Scott, born in Monroe County in 1874, recalled working as a "grown man for fifteen cents a day. When I got to making forty to fifty cents a day, I thought I was getting rich."

NON-FARMING OCCUPATIONS

Between 1870 and 1930 the financial plight was alleviated for some families whose menfolk began working in area logging and sawmilling activities; as seasonal raftsmen on the Cumberland, Caney Fork, Obey, Roaring, or Wolf rivers; in the lucrative sandstone industry associated with the beautiful multicolored patterns of Crab Orchard quartzite; or as coal miners on portions of the Cumberland Plateau. All these activities were ideally suited for unskilled labor, thus making feasible the idea of dividing time between farming activities on the one hand and working for pay on the other. These wages provided the men with their only means of buying staple items for use at home.

The logging-rafting occupation that developed comprised men of both races who farmed a little on the side. Some of them turned agricultural activities over to their wives and children and devoted full attention to cutting logs from their own boundaries or working as loggers for larger landowners and timber buyers. Most men of the area, regardless of social class, willingly defied the rain-swollen creeks and rivers at one time or another. Others became famous in local circles when their physical feats and prowess provided grist for stories at all sorts of social gatherings. Many of these accounts blossomed into legends that are still told up and down the Cumberland and its major tributaries.

Chief among the legend-makers was Bob Riley, one of the first raft pilots to make the run all the way down the Cumberland from Celina to Nashville. He grew up at Fox Springs, a rural community located near the mouth of Mitchell Creek on the Obey River. Although Riley was reputedly one of the best pilots to run rafts on the Cumberland, his chief claim to fame stems from his prowess as a forager while en route. One of the Riley legends, retold by his daughter Rachel Langford, explains how he conned a farm woman out of a fat turkey:

His raft had been torn apart near the bank and was being repaired. . . . He spied a large flock of turkeys in a farm yard. [He got in a canoe that was tied to the raft and] paddled to the bank.

He singled out a goodly-sized gobbler and began chasing it around the farm yard. The wife of the house, hearing the commotion, came out and demanded an explanation: "Why are you chasing my turkey?"

Bob answered very quickly in a tearful voice and told of their plight of hunger. They had brought a turkey from Celina and aimed to eat him, Riley told

A sawmill in Pickett County, 1972 (Photo by David Sutherland)

her. "But this morning he picked the knot untied and joined your flock. Won't you please help me catch him?"

The lady gladly helped him catch one of her turkeys. The turkey was cooked, and the hungry raftsmen had a feast.

On the next trip down the river, Bob stopped and explained the truth [to the woman] and more than paid her for the worth of the turkey.

Some of the men who spent time in the logging-rafting industry and earned niches in local legendry went on to achieve regional and national recognition in other fields. John J. Gore became a U. S. district judge; Monroe County-born Benton McMillan moved to Tennessee and was later elected as governor of that state; and Cordell Hull of Pickett County was serving as secretary of state under Franklin Roosevelt when Hull initiated proceedings that led to the founding of the United Nations.

Understanding the timber industry of the Upper Cumberland region means comprehending that the term *folk industry* refers to a locally owned operation. While northern entrepreneurs were gobbling up large acreages of forested land and mineral rights in southern Appalachia for a mere fraction of their actual worth, most owners of forest-covered lands in the Upper Cumberland clung tenaciously to their private tracts. In so doing, they remained in charge of their economic destiny. The folk of the Upper Cumberland retained control of their own hardwood industry during the rafting era (1870–1930), and they continue to do so at the present time by maintaining ownership and management of area sawmills and timber processing plants. The Homer Bartley Lumber Company has a paid ad that is aired over a Glasgow radio station and promises the highest available prices for standing timber. I am reminded when I hear this radio commercial that I attended a one-room school with Bobby Bartley (present and third-generation owner-operator of the lumber company) when his father Homer Bartley was a young man just getting started in the logging and sawmilling business.

The region's timber industry continues to be a folk enterprise dominated by farmer-loggers and modest milling operations. In the words of folklorist-geographer Steven A. Schulman, "It is impossible to separate the logging industry of the [Upper] Cumberland from the folklife of the area, because of the involvement of the local people in the business."

Coal mining was at one time another important economic enterprise in certain portions of the region, constituting a major source of employment for numerous men during the early-to-mid years of the twentieth century. Women, too, worked in the mines, especially those that were family-owned and -operated.

Mining activity along the western edge of the Cumberland Plateau on the Fentress-Overton county border, and in eastern Fentress near Armathwaite, dates from the mid-nineteenth century when occupants of nearby hollows occasionally dug a few bushels of coal and hauled it to their homes where it was mixed with wood for domestic fuel. George A. Knight writes in *My Album of Memories* that, while the presence of coal here was a well-known fact in scientific and commercial circles, most residents of the area were unaware of the economic significance of the coal.

Unlike the situation in local timber industry, the origins of mine ownership in the Fentress-Overton area, for example, can be traced to the northern entrepreneurs who snatched up the land in astonishingly large chunks, mainly during the late years of the nineteenth century. "Before they came, land wasn't worth ten cents an acre," Crawford resident Coyle Copeland observed. "It was often swapped for a pig or a horse."

The first of these outsiders to take up land in the area was John B. McCormick, an industrial magnate, who purchased five thousand acres from the state of Tennessee in the 1880s and later sold it to Elizabeth Manning of Queens, New York. The Manning heirs accumulated a much larger estate before selling to the A. J. Crawford syndicate at the turn of the century. The Crawford enterprise began exploring for coal about the same time that the Nashville-Knoxville Railroad built a spur line from Monterey to Hanging Limb, and Jere Baxter and other officials of the Tennessee Central Railroad were formulating plans to build their own railroad from Nashville to Knoxville. Because of the presence of thick coal seams in the Crawford-Davidson-Twinton-Wilder areas, mining and railroad representatives believed that Cookeville, Crossville, and Harriman to the east would form the nucleus of heavy industry, turning this portion of the Upper Cumberland into another Pittsburgh or Birmingham.

Representatives of these companies "came to the Wilder-Davidson area in 1896 with a satchelful of money and a batch of lawyers to purchase ninety-nine-year leases for railroad right-of-way," Copeland claimed. "Most of the people here had never seen a hundred-dollar bill," he went on. "So they bought some of the land; stole some of the land."

Stimulated by these developments, former Union army general John T. Wilder purchased thousands of acres of Fentress County land between 1902 and 1906. Not long afterwards, he sold out to the Nashville-based Fentress Coal and Coke Company and left the area. However, his name remained affixed to the new community of Wilder. In the meantime, the Tennessee Central extended its Monterey-Crawford spur line all the way to Wilder, where huge coal deposits signalled a rarely matched mining enterprise. By 1920, local mining villages on the plateau boasted of recreation parks, hotels, schools, churches, family dwellings, bunk-houses, and mess halls.

When the first mine opened near Crawford in 1902, the workday was eleven hours long and the daily wage was $1.25. By 1912, however, efforts to improve living conditions at Crawford and the miners' quest for an eight-hour workday led to the formation of a labor union thought to have been a chapter of the Knights of Labor. This local union folded in 1914 because the company blacklisted the strikers and would not permit them to return to the mine.

A new movement to organize the miners came about during World War I when coal was in heavy demand and mining operations were booming everywhere in the country. In 1917, miners at Davidson, Twinton, and Wilder were unionized by the United Mine Workers of America and achieved a wage scale of $3.20 per day, and that amount increased annually. But when an economic depression hit the coal market in 1921 and 1922, the local coal operators reduced the wage scale to the original $3.20. Eventually, all mining operations were halted in an effort to destroy organized resistance.

The mines operated on an open-shop basis between the years 1924 and 1931. In order to work during that period, those who made applications to work in the mines had to sign "yellow-dog" contracts, vowing in writing that they would never join a union or go out on strike. These contracts were negated by the miners in 1931, however, when the mine owners and operators once again sought to cut wages because of economic pressures brought about by the Great Depression. The only recourse left to the miners was a new union contract with the UMW, which went into effect at mid-year in 1931.

When the new contract expired on July 8, 1932, the miners were still suffering financially. The coal operators refused to grant a cost-of-living wage increase on the grounds that such a concession would wreck their mining enterprises. Without a union to bargain for them, between six hundred and eight hundred miners were out of work. The mines remained closed through the rest of that summer.

When the Fentress Coal and Coke Company reopened the Wilder mine in October 1932, using imported "scabs" (strikebreakers), pandemonium and lawlessness reigned supreme. In the weeks that followed, railroad tracks, bridges, and trestles were dynamited or burned, and Tennessee state militiamen, ordered in by a governor under political pressure, were to be seen everywhere with their pistols, rifles, bayonets, and machine guns.

Killings, dynamitings, burnings, and robberies were daily occurrences throughout the winter and spring. The final blow against the destitute miners came on the night of April 29, 1933, when their leader and hero, Barney Graham, was gunned down on the streets of Wilder. The starving miners had now lost both the war and their persuasive leader. The future held no hope at all. Defeat, gloom, and utter pessimism engulfed them.

For all practical purposes, large-scale mining activities were never resumed. Various other companies continued to extract coal from the area throughout the 1950s but in diminished volume. Today, the old coal mining communities in the Fentress-Overton area are economically depressed. Most present residents draw miners' pensions, black lung benefits, or social security. The five or six remaining dwellings located in Davidson are in advanced stages of decay; there is not a single building left in Wilder. "People come through here now and they can't believe it when I tell them that there was a whole town down there," said an unidentified source quoted in an article by Fran Ansley and Brenda Bell. "There was thousands of people there then." Ironically, the Wilder post office was moved to Davidson, which is now identified as Wilder on road maps.

Over the years coal was also extracted from deposits in other portions of the Upper Cumberland, especially at Zenith, located in eastern

Fentress County, and near Sparta, where the mine opened there in 1836 supplied local coal needs for fifty years. Other mines in White County caused it to rank high among Tennessee's coal producers by 1920.

Shaft mining has also occurred since Civil War days in Kentucky on the banks of the Big South Fork River near the Wayne-McCreary County border. In earlier times, miners there hauled coal out of the mines in mule-drawn cars over short tramlines that extended from the mines to the river. They dumped coal into wooden barges that were sent downstream to Burnside when rains afforded the river with a "coal boat tide."

In more recent times, strip mining has come to the Upper Cumberland. But it was from the earlier mining operations that narratives, community legends, ballads, and satirical prose came, generated by persons who had often witnessed events firsthand.

Though coal mining in Fentress County was not the primary reason for an influx of German settlers there during the late years of the nineteenth century, it soon played a part in their destiny. At the same time that mining began in the Wilder-Crawford-Twinton area, Bruno Gernt, a German-born resident of Michigan and land agent for the Clarke family of Nebraska, was making plans to build a model city just east of Jamestown.

Gernt first saw the plateau land of Fentress County in 1879 and immediately envisioned a town laid out geometrically with parcels set aside for schools, churches, and businesses. Land was to be sold in parcels of twenty-five, fifty, and two hundred acres. It would be no trouble, he felt, to attract hundreds of German immigrants to this pristine area where the soil and other natural resources would make them entirely self-sufficient. And with rapid railroad expansion taking place elsewhere in the South, Gernt recognized the potential for industrial development as well.

Gernt named this model city for his friend and partner M. H. Allardt, who died just as plans for the settlement were getting under way. Although the German immigrants developed an excellent agricultural enterprise in and around Allardt, with products being shipped to northern markets and to Europe, Gernt still dreamed of industry—coal mines, factories, and railroads. Drilling private test wells, he led Fentress County into the oil business and helped pioneer coal and lumber industries as well.

Gernt's dream of industry went unfulfilled, however, as he was never able to attract a railroad into the immediate area. Many of the German settlers who had relocated in Fentress County left during and just after World War I, moving away to more prosperous areas, especially to Cincinnati, from which a number had come.

It may be that public sentiment against the local German element was partly responsible for the exodus. A letter from Gerald W. Gernt,

Bruno's great-grandson, dated June 6, 1992, points to this possibility. He notes that Bruno Gernt immediately instituted a public school, probably taught in English. Because of the brevity of the school year, however, Gernt recruited Max Colditz to teach his eight children as well as other children in the area, sometimes at night. Gerald Gernt believes that Colditz taught these classes in German. "I do know that World War I ended the German influence in public schools and that most of the children after that time were told not to speak German in public," writes Gernt. "As late as the early 1950s I remember German being spoken in private homes among family members."

Local feelings about those of German ancestry may not have been too negative, however, as quite a few of the founding families stayed on to engage in mining practices and the lucrative timber industry in portions of Fentress, Scott, and Morgan counties. Many of them are buried there. Their progeny still live in the Allardt-Jamestown area today, taking considerable pride in their German heritage.

THE REGION'S AFRICAN AMERICAN HERITAGE

Although African Americans were participants in the various economic activities described above, just when the majority of them came to the Upper Cumberland is not known. Documentation exists showing that some of the white pioneers of the early 1800s brought along a few slaves. Ernest Lawson writes that there were 1,268 slaves in Cumberland County, Kentucky, in 1840, with a listed value of $440,000. He noted that Burkesville became a slave-trading center replete with slave auctions on the courthouse grounds. My own study of the black Coe settlement in the southern portion of that county points out that slaves were brought in as early as 1811 and that, according to oral testimonials, slave auctions were indeed conducted on the public square in Burkesville.

Ownership of two to four slaves was fairly common across the region. Nonetheless, all of Kentucky's Upper Cumberland counties were Unionist in sentiment during the Civil War, as were most of those on the Tennessee side of the line. Kink Strode of Monroe County was representative of the Union sympathizers before and during the war who were both Union soldiers and slaveholders. Family tradition reports that he commented after the war, "I was not aware that I was fighting to free my own two slaves, Jane and Isom, until I was right in the middle of the Battle of Shiloh." Jane and Isom continued on with Strode after freedom and were buried alongside their former master and mistress in the Strode family cemetery.

Oral traditional history of slavery times in the region does not neglect instances of cruelty and inhumane treatment accorded slaves by some white masters. On the whole, however, the worst feature of slavery here was the simple fact that one person was held in servitude by another and thus viewed as chattel. Oral recollections among blacks typically indicate that there was little observable difference between their ancestors' living conditions during slavery times and the period of freedom that followed. Often, they continued to live as sharecroppers or renters in the same structures they had occupied as slaves, farming the same land and tending the same vegetable gardens.

Continued existence on the land was sometimes impossible for land-owners and slaves alike, especially when the owners had gone away to war to fight for the southern cause. Fentress County historian Albert Hogue, who was born shortly after the Civil War ended, claimed that the pine groves there now cover large tracts of land once farmed by slaves. "Their masters went away to fight for the South, and were afraid to return," he wrote. When the slaves were freed, the ex-Unionists, now in control of the local courts, used their legal authority to prevent the return of the white landowners. Murder indictments were secured against the former slaveholders for killings that allegedly occurred during the war, and lands were attached to satisfy these charges. The scared landholders never returned to make a defense, Hogue stated; thus the civil suits were decided against them. Their slaves often followed them to other lands and left no one to cultivate the fields.

In numerous instances across the region, ex-slave families who chose to remain in rural settings after they were freed maintained a high degree of contact with white neighbors. It was not uncommon, however, to hear a white person use the term 'darkies" when referring to black people. That disparaging term was used, for example, in the Celina newspaper around 1900 to describe local people of color.

All things considered, however, racial harmony existed in most communities across the region, and the sharing of cultural forms such as music, stories, beliefs, foodways, and weather prophesies occurred in an admirable manner. Interracial friendships carved out back then, along with positive feelings resulting from the efforts of each race to be helpful to the other, often carried over to the present generations.

The situation in the Martins Creek community along the Jackson-Putnam border attests to the harmony enjoyed by white families and black families who lived there from slavery times to the 1930s and sometimes beyond. Ralph Maddux and his sister Martha Breeding told of the numerous African American families residing on Martins Creek when they were young adults in the 1930s. Many were still there when Ralph went off to war, he said, but when he returned in the mid-1940s after five years in the military, individual blacks who remained behind could be counted on one's fingers.

Sara Coe Tooley of Ft. Run, Monroe County, who grew up in the Coe Ridge Colony (Photo by the author)

They had "gone below," Martha added, quoting the expression used by area residents of African descent, meaning that they had moved away to places such as Carthage, Lebanon, Gallatin, Cookeville, Nashville, or Chattanooga, as well as to out-of-state urban areas. Her comment prompted Ralph to recall with humor the time he ran into a former black neighbor who had moved to Carthage:

One Saturday morning I was over at Carthage at the produce house, and I saw a black man there that I knew. I remembered him but he didn't remember me. I walked over to him and said, "Hello Jack."

And he said, "Hello there."

And I said, "How are you getting along?"

He said, "I'm doing good."

And I said, "Jack, you don't know who I am, do you?"

Then he said, "No, sir, I don't know who you are, but you sure do favor yourself."

Maddux then observed that most of the older blacks had remained behind on Martins Creek, that it was the younger ones who had left in quest of "greener pastures." Very few members of the black Sadlers left the area, however. Three Sadler families, along with a Montgomery family, were tenant farmers on the Dr. Freeman place there on the creek. Gordon King Sadler, one of the black Sadlers who did leave Martins Creek for a new beginning in Gallatin, visited in the Ralph Maddux home in mid-1991. He still referred to the place on Martins Creek where he had grown up as "home." Twenty-five to thirty of his siblings and ancestors are interred in their own cemetery there.

One of the Sadlers buried there is Uncle Med, who is still remembered for the three items he kept under his bed at all times: a washpan full of water to drown his troubles, an axe with the blade turned upward to cut body pain, and a shotgun to keep away evil spirits. Med also served as a weather prophet. It is said that in the event of a drouth, he would kill a snake and tie it to a tree in order to predict rain. If its body turned in a certain direction, rain would come soon.

Through the 1930s the Martins Creek blacks, along with several black families from nearby Granville, held an annual picnic on Spring Ford Creek—an event that featured barbequed goat and old-time dance music played by members of the Sadler family. The goat, purchased with money contributed by some of the black families, was served free of charge at the picnic. It was barbequed by Uncle Case Sadler, Med's brother.

Many of the counties in the Upper Cumberland had African American enclaves to which numerous ex-slaves gravitated. Some counties had three or four such settlements, some even up to a dozen. Wayne County, Kentucky, appears to be unique in having had a dozen or so rural black communities during the period between the Civil War and World War II. Much of the clustering there as elsewhere across the region resulted from the freed people's desire to go it alone, "to forge a community based on economic security and self-determination," write folklorists Elizabeth Peterson and Tom Rankin in describing the early residents of Free Hill in Clay County. Typically, the lands occupied by the ex-slaves had been sold to them or donated by their former owners.

There were isolated instances of Ku Klux Klan activities across the region in early years, as well as unrelated acts of violence and terrorist threats against local black individuals and families. Sporadic racial threats and incidents of brutality occurred in all parts of the Upper Cumberland from the late nineteenth century through the 1930s, often causing black people to leave the area. In 1940, Lewis D. Bandy of Macon County offered the following explanation as to why no black people were located in Lafayette, the county seat:

The population in Macon County in 1860 was: White, 5,244; Negro, 1,046. . . . This had changed by 1930 to White, 13,559 and Negro 313. . . .

The above tells a story within itself as far as the race problem is concerned. The Negro has almost entirely left the county to the white. It was never a county suited to slavery; after being freed, a great many of the slaves drifted on to other sections; and the two races were never able to get along together. This leads to the relating of an unpleasant incident that happened in the Negro [section] of Lafayette about thirty-five years ago.

There had been trouble among the Negro population. A white man had been murdered. The accused Negro was taken from jail on bond one night and started home. Before he had gone very far, many shots rang out and the body was found riddled with bullets. Sometime later, with feelings still not settled, every Negro house in Lafayette was blasted one night. Since that time, there has never been a Negro home located within the town, or near it. It is even now a rare thing to see a Negro on the streets—after sundown, especially.

Research for the present volume indicates that indeed no African American families presently reside in Lafayette; neither are there any black students currently enrolled in Macon County High School. Indications are that the county as a whole, like Cumberland County, Tennessee, to the east, has virtually no black inhabitants.

The Beginnings of a New Era

For blacks and whites alike, the 1920s brought needed improvements in education, along with the introduction of numerous new industries—cheese plants, creameries, fruit and vegetable canneries, and poultry- and fruit-shipping centers. Area farm families sorely needed the economic benefits made possible by these farm-to-market enterprises. Small dairy herds became commonplace across the region, fruit-growing and fruit nursery stock cultivation increased in some counties, and poultry production turned into a real business for some families rather than merely providing "egg money" for farm wives.

The economic surge of the mid-1920s notwithstanding, many men from the Upper Cumberland, especially those who were not employed in the logging, rafting, or mining industries, chose to leave their hill country farms for work in the industrial cities of central and northern Illinois, Indiana, and Ohio. Sometimes entire families, both blacks and whites, left the region for what promised to be a better life for all concerned. There were some departures, especially among blacks, as early as the 1890s; on the whole, however, out-migration from the Upper Cumberland did not begin until the 1920s.

(My own father's movements to and from the region provide an illustration of the migration pattern. Montell left his home in the Mt. Gilead community of north central Monroe County in 1925 for South Bend, Indiana, where he worked at the Studebaker plant. Dissatisfied with his decision, he returned home about a year later and married Hazel Chapman from the nearby Rock Bridge community. But financial stress once again sent him northward, this time to Toledo, Ohio. He was employed at an automotive factory when the Great Depression hit in 1929. Preferring the emotional security of farm life and home back in Kentucky, Montell left the city and returned to Monroe County.)

Ascertaining when the old ways of life ended in the Upper Cumberland and modern times began is difficult, since change was occurring all along. The introduction of improved agricultural technology in the 1870s and 1880s was a portent, although at the beginning of the twentieth century there were still no automobiles, airplanes, radios, or electricity and very few telephones. Families were still largely self-sufficient, growing their own food and making their own clothing and furniture. The few items not available at home were obtained from a small community store reached by foot or on horseback. News of friends and others in the community was picked up there or during monthly attendance at church.

The presence of crank-box telephone systems, banks, silent-movie houses, automobiles, and a few road improvements made between 1900 and 1930 did not yet herald a new way of life. The same kinds of agricultural implements introduced in the 1880s were still in use in the late 1930s. Parents and children alike were often underdressed. All too many of them knew what it was like to stand in line for government handouts of food and clothing.

Ward Curtis of north central Monroe County described that experience in the following oral account:

The government started a relief program at Persimon, the first that I know of. I walked the five or six miles to get there. They give away commodities, groceries, canned goods. I got a two-bushel meal sack full of canned goods besides all I could hold in my arms and what I could put in my pockets. And I put all that on my back and started home.

A fellow followed me out onto the porch and he said, "Man, leave that here; that will kill you. Leave that here and go somewhere and get you a mule to take that home. To tell you the truth, I wouldn't want one of my mules to carry it," he said.

But I come on about a mile, or a mile and a half—come to where my brother-in-law lived. I just thought that I could leave some of that there. So I left part of it there and I brought the rest of it home.

Then the next place that they were giving it away was out on the road about two and a half miles from my house. I went and got three sacks of flour—three twenty-five-pound sacks. I put that flour on my shoulder, all three sacks, and carried it home on my shoulder.

I wasn't a bit rested when I got home, but a fellow was proud to get that flour back then. I would have carried it ten miles I guess, or at least would have tried.

Well, my wife heard that they had dresses to give away. And she wanted me to go and get her a new dress. I went and caught the old mule and got on it and went out. Another neighbor joined in with me to go get his wife a new dress.

We went out there and stood in line for half a day. Finally, he got in, got his wife a dress. I went in, but they didn't have one for my wife. And we started home and got within about a mile or a little over of home. We separated there.

And I was so cold that I thought I would get off and drive my old mule. I got off but the old mule just humped up and she wouldn't go. And I had to get back on that old mule and I nearly froze to death.

When I got home I told my wife to get me a pan of water—hot water—right quick, that my fingers were froze. She got me a pan of water and when I stuck my hand down in that pan of water, I cried. Just like a baby. Just seemed like my fingernails were coming off.

When I finally did get warm, I told her, says, "A woman would send a man to hell to get a new dress."

"Well," she says, "I wouldn't mind going."

"Well," I says, "you can go the next time."

Well, the next time she heard they had them dresses, she lit out. She had to go up on some big steps; stand on a big platform up there. And if it had fell, no telling how many it would have hurt. Maybe it could have killed some of them. She stood up there for awhile, too proud to stand there for people to look at.

She got down from there and come home. She said, "If I never get a new dress 'til I go and stand up there for everybody to look at, I'll never get one."

So I says, "I thought you thought it was funny." But she never did ask me to go back and get her a dress. And I never asked to go either.

Not content to live off government relief programs, nor to accommodate the fear that such might one day be their fate, many area families looked elsewhere for work and a better life; thus out-migration continued apace during the Great Depression. Even when that traumatic decade came to a close, people continued to leave the Upper Cumberland for Indianapolis, Muncie, Detroit, Chicago, Peoria, Cincinnati, and other industrial locations when word would come from a relative or friend with news that "a job is waiting for you here. Come on up."

The stream of migrants from the region flowed as a mighty river during the 1940s and 1950s. Clay and Jackson counties, for example, sustained approximately 40 percent drops in population during that twenty-year period, including virtually all members of the black race. Most of them were tenant farmers who did not make enough each year from the sale of crops to pay off their grocery store debts.

James Armstrong, a black resident of the Tick community just north of Gainesboro, mentioned the time he went to Indianapolis to find work.

"How long did you stay there?" I asked.

"All night," he responded, tongue in cheek.

Armstrong wanted nothing to do with strange urban living, but he commented that his brother who moved to Indianapolis worked there until he died.

Gainesboro had enough black families still residing there as late as the 1930s to justify the erection and maintenance of a "colored school" for its eighty to ninety black students. In 1991, Annie Williams was the only remaining black person in Gainesboro and one of about a half-dozen blacks who still resided in Jackson County.

The Depression years came to a close with the eruption of World War II. Farm prices in the Upper Cumberland rose sharply and area residents who had remained at home and weathered the throes of the Great Depression benefited accordingly. It was now possible for the younger members of a family to attend a Western movie each Saturday at the county seat, as well as to enjoy a bag of popcorn, hamburger, and a "cold drink" (the usual term for a cola or other soft drink). Such delightful commodities were available through the war years at a total cost of thirty-five cents or less at most county seats. Those same youngsters grown up recall some of the unpleasant impacts the war had on homelife, however, as many items such as sugar and gasoline were rationed and thus available only with government coupons.

Agricultural practices assumed a new look during the post-war years. Thanks to the efforts of county agricultural agents across the region, farmers sold their horses and mules, purchased tractors, introduced better varieties of fruit, hay, corn, and new grain crops, and replaced low-priced dark tobacco with burley. Though large and diversified, agriculture remained an industry that continued to hold families and communities together.

The years during and immediately after the war saw unprecedented change in folklife in the Upper Cumberland. Soldiers came home with new ideas about life, living, and family, as did some of the men and women who had worked out of the region in strategic defense industries. Many of these sons and daughters chose to leave their farms and small towns in favor of city life, both in and out of the region. Cookeville and Somerset profited some in this regard, but it was Nashville and Chattanooga, along with the large midwestern urban centers previously named, that were the heavy winners. Population declined drastically across the region. Virtually every county had two to three thousand fewer people in 1970 than in 1940.

In a conversation I had with Sam Anderson, mayor of Gainesboro, he said, "See those trees over there on that first ridge?" He pointed across Cordell Hull Lake.

I nodded in the affirmative as I viewed the dense stand of timber. "Does the land now belong to the corps?" I asked.

"No, it's private property," Anderson responded. "The owners moved out! Just left it behind."

"A lot of the land in Jackson County has been acquired by out-of-

region people, or regional urban dwellers, as a tax write-off," added Anderson's wife, Katherine. "They've just allowed it to grow up in timber."

Sisters in eastern Wayne County, 1975 (Photo by the author)

Thanks to the coming of the Army Corps of Engineers dams, beginning with Dale Hollow in 1943, flooding was no longer a problem for the small towns of the area, and low-cost electricity became available to many rural homes. It was not until the early 1950s, however, that electricity and its accompanying amenities were accessible to all farm families.

The four major dams in the region (Dale Hollow, Wolf Creek, Center Hill, and Cordell Hull) created a gigantic sportsman's paradise that is immensely popular with fishermen, boat enthusiasts, water-skiers, and nature lovers. This system of lakes annually delights thousands of tourists who visit the region but also saddens the hearts of countless displaced people who can never go home again. While the presence of these four lakes has benefited the Upper Cumberland, both economically and culturally, there has also been a negative side: the rafting industry on the Cumberland River was destroyed, and other disruptive factors contributed to the break-up of families and the end of a way of life.

Because of the availability of cheap electricity, a large female labor force, and the absence of labor unions across the Upper Cumberland, clothing factories were built in just about every county seat town and sizeable village in the area during the 1950s. Counties, towns, factories, and families alike prospered. Of the eleven counties in Tennessee's Upper Cumberland in 1940, only Putnam and White could boast of more than two hundred employees in the apparel industry. Collectively, the others had only 116 persons working in clothing factories that year. Thirty years later, in 1970, garment factory employment in the eleven counties combined totalled 11,393. In 1980, 11,013 persons still worked in the garment plants, but seven of the counties registered a net loss of clothing apparel jobs ranging upward to a staggering 35 percent in Smith County.

With the coming of factories to the region, most families benefited from the heretofore unknown luxury of a regular pay check. This time around, however, it was a woman's world. It was they who primarily went to work in these plants. Married women with children left their husbands at home to baby-sit, farm a little, or perhaps work at part-time jobs.

In contrast, payroll checks had long been a part of life for townspeople. Most of them had worked over the years as store clerks, at local sawmills or handle factories, or in service-type jobs, where only a few persons could be hired. Farmers seldom sought employment in such places until the 1930s and thereafter, as the lack of roads and transportation made daily commuting difficult. Clinton County, which was typical, had only two miles of paved roads in 1919. In the mid-1930s, Opal Smith noted in her Federal Writers Project report that the industrial base of Albany, county seat of Clinton, consisted only of a flour mill, grist mill, dogwood mill, and a hickory mill that specialized in handles.

In Tennessee, Cumberland County experienced spectacular growth in the 1930s with the establishment of Cumberland Homesteads, a government rehabilitation project prompted by Eleanor Roosevelt. As a result, 28,000 acres were set aside to serve agricultural needs of the families moving into the 250 houses constructed of Crab Orchard stone. Cumberland County's population grew appreciably during the 1970s and 1980s, thanks to an influx of out-of-region retirees looking for a temperate climate and a slower pace.

Garment factories, rehabilitation projects, retirement villages, and other economic factors notwithstanding, the Upper Cumberland went through a series of years marked by low employment. In 1975, when the region had a 9.9 percent jobless rate, community leaders recognized the urgency of attracting more industry to complement the old but healthy timber-related industries and the equally healthy more recent tourist and clothing industries. Failure to attract new and diversified industries to the region would mean a continued loss of the native labor force to other geographical areas. These efforts were generally successful, however, as most counties in the Upper Cumberland registered a net increase in jobs and population in both 1980 and 1990.

Of the total population of the entire Upper Cumberland area in 1990, approximately 98.0 percent were white and 1.5 percent black. This is the way demographic matters have stood since the 1930s, when many black people departed the scene permanently. The lack of distribution equity is striking: most black people in Tennessee's Upper Cumberland now live in Alexandria and Dowelltown in DeKalb County, Algood in Putnam County, Carthage in Smith County, and Sparta in White County.

Of the few blacks in Kentucky's Upper Cumberland at the beginning of the 1990s, most were located in the county seat towns in small enclaves that once were typically given such racist names as "Nigger Kingdom" or "Nigger Hill." Such sections still exist in most towns, but there is more mixing of the races in these poor neighborhoods than in past years. For example, Tompkinsville still has its "kingdom" (the racial prefix is typically no longer included), along with a place called Milltown that once served as a buffer between kingdom residents and adjacent whites. Milltown was typically occupied by lower-class blacks and whites alike who were often frowned upon by both races. It is said that the residents of Milltown often cohabited, sold illegal whiskey, ran houses of prostitution, engaged in street brawling, and generally provided local police with adequate work. Blacks and whites often live next to each other now, perhaps drawn together by shared economic conditions that leave much to be desired.

Old Order Amish and Mennonites, newcomers to the Upper Cumberland, have been arriving generally since the mid-1970s. Settlements of these highly respected people of the soil are scattered across the region, providing their mainstream neighbors with glimpses into a way of life they themselves or their progenitors once knew. Neither Amish nor Mennonites count their members individually, being concerned instead with the total number of families in a settlement or colony.

African Americans and persons of European ancestry now residing in the Upper Cumberland have all inherited and spawned various beliefs, customs, practices, institutions, and peculiar ways of thinking and acting that continue to enrich their lives. Some of these traditions are hoary with age; some have been created within the recent past. Some are esoteric, serving only the needs of a particular individual, family, or community. However, much of the region's folklore is shared by people of all races and nationalities. Whatever a tradition's age or distribution, it often constitutes a vital voice of the present, to be called on in appropriate social, cultural, and economic situations. By understanding the nature of regional folklore and folklife, one can better understand the totality of area life and culture—how things came to be as they are. The subsequent chapters are designed to illuminate these folk cultural aspects of the historic Upper Cumberland region.

The Old Way of Life and New Beginnings

As people in the communities of the Upper Cumberland worked both individually and collectively to achieve self-sufficiency, several societal institutions developed with varying degrees of complexity. Here as elsewhere the family unit formed the basis of life's chief concerns. All other social forces served largely to reinforce the strength of the family, whose members viewed daily work as a prerequisite for survival. Concern for the soul and the mind led to the establishment of churches and schools, and the need for physical well-being promoted and perpetuated recreational and medicinal practices.

All of these social institutions fostered community interaction. Church activities promoted fellowship, and the schools provided intellectual stimulus for children and entertainment for all in the form of spelling bees, ciphering matches, and pie suppers. Children and adults alike gathered for group games and dances, and home remedies and treatments were constantly exchanged among neighbors. In all regards the family and the community at large reinforced and supported each other in good times and in bad.

These major institutions were and are significant tradition-bearers, perpetuating customs originated by pioneer settlers. Today, they serve as historical indicators of a people's needs and their progress in meeting those needs, individually and collectively.

Folklife and Self-Sufficiency

Making things by hand has been an integral part of area folklife activity since the late 1700s. Folklife scholars point out that traditional folk crafts often combine functional and decorative elements, and that the utilitarian aspect of these crafts—their usefulness—ties them most clearly to historical times. In *Seedtime on the Cumberland* and *Flowering of the Cumberland*, Harriette Simpson Arnow chronicled certain facets of the early history of the region, paying special attention to the importance of practical skills in everyday life. She observed that the first settlers used skills they had learned traditionally, along with intuitive knowledge, to fill basic needs with materials near at hand. The pioneer era encouraged widespread proficiency in many kinds of handwork.

The self-sufficiency that characterized life on the Upper Cumberland frontier persisted well into the twentieth century in some parts of the region, where rugged terrain and relative isolation kept many families reliant on subsistence farming, hunting, fishing, musselling (for buttons and pearls), making whiskey, and forest-related livelihoods. Economic conditions created trends toward specialization in some crafts among families and individuals during the early years of the nineteenth century, and this situation continues in the present. Traditional ways of making can be seen in the construction of human dwellings and animal shelters.

FOLK ARCHITECTURE

"The Little Old Log Cabin in the Lane," a song written by Will S. Hays, crystallized the nostalgic feelings held by many nineteenth-century residents of the Upper Cumberland. Most of the region's people of that day had personal (if not fond) memories of life in a small log cabin constructed of native materials. Capt. J. R. Copeland of Livingston, born in 1806, wrote in later years that he "was here in the days of log cabins and puncheon floors—yes, and puncheon tables, for I first ate at a table that was made of board puncheons put upon legs."

People who could not testify personally to this sort of experience needed only to recall the testimonies of parents and grandparents. George Carver, for example, built a log cabin in the Hegira community of Cumberland County, Kentucky, during the early 1800s. The kitchen, a separate building located a few feet away from the main cabin, had only a bare earth floor for the first few years after construction. It was here that family members gathered to "sit on the floor and warm by the fireplace." In the yard stood two very large chestnut stumps. Carver family tradition holds that each was hollowed out, one to serve as a smokehouse, the other as shelter for the hogs.

Nowhere in the country was the geography more suited to log construction than in the wooded landscape of the Upper Cumberland. One- or two-room structures, along with the other buildings that made up the total farmstead, were placed in every conceivable topographic location, although higher elevations were the most popular. Barns were not necessarily built on a lower elevation than human dwellings, but such an arrangement did prevent drainage from the barn area from polluting the family's water supply. Most dwellings were erected close to a free-flowing spring that generally originated in a bluff cave. The spring had to be large enough to provide water for all household needs, including refrigeration of food and dairy products. Often, spring water was all that was available for watering draft animals and other livestock.

Folk architecture in the Upper Cumberland exhibits the skills of local builders who were craftsmen in their own right, and who often employed the same tools as those who made baskets, chairs, handles, and other objects. Early cabin homes in the Upper Cumberland, occupied by farmers and villagers alike, were square or slightly rectangular and typically had only one room. When more privacy was needed, two rooms were created by dividing the first with a non-weight-bearing partition. Cabins had only a loft above the main level, but later one- and two-room structures called for a half-story sleeping area upstairs, reached by means of a narrow, steep, boxed-in stairway located near the fireplace. In early times, a ladder fastened against the interior wall often provided access to such an area.

These frontier homes served as food storage areas as well as living quarters. Dried foods such as beans, corn, pumpkins, and other home-grown items would hang from nails on the upstairs ceiling beams. Onions and potatoes were stored in the loft area. During cold weather, it was common practice to add an additional layer of cover to these items every time one was added to the beds occupied by people. In early spring, as occupants discarded each quilt or blanket, a corresponding one would be removed from the onions and potatoes.

The roofs of these folk houses typically extended beyond the exterior

A Fentress County log house, 1972. The roofline extends outward to shield the step-shouldered stone chimney. (Photo by David Sutherland)

wall at the chimney end so as to enclose the chimney itself. This traditional construction feature, known also among the Cherokee of western North Carolina, sufficiently shielded the early stick-and-clay chimneys from the ravages of wind, rain, and snow. The clay was thus prevented from softening and falling away from the chimney's woody portions (which consisted of short logs). With the clay gone, the wood often ignited and burned the entire structure. Later chimneys were erected of native limestone or sandstone that was available nearby in stratified layers, especially in the numerous creekbeds that traversed the area. However, the roofline, covered with hand-riven white oak shingles, still protruded beyond the chimney in most instances. This is a prime example of a cultural tradition that is continued simply because "this is the way it was always done."

The pioneers seldom thought of log buildings as "pretty," and they took whatever measures were available to hide the logs. Lena Moss Blaydes of Metcalfe County recalled a family story describing how her ancestors found deposits of "blue mud," mixed it with water until it had a paint-like consistency, and applied it to the log exteriors with rags. She also stated that "burnt umber served as paint. It was mixed with linseed oil, and produced dark red, brown, or black color." Sarah Jane Crabtree Koger, who was born near Jamestown, Tennessee, related how when she was a child in the 1890s her family covered the log interiors with white muslin stretched from wall to wall.

A house style featuring two equal-sized log rooms built around a central chimney came into vogue during the early years of the nineteenth century. This common dwelling is identified as a "saddlebag" house by folklorists and others, but most local folk referred to it simply as a "story-and-a-half" house, meaning that the upper-level living space was only a half-story tall at the eaves.

In another type of folk structure of similar vintage the two living units were divided by an open breezeway or "dogtrot." Sometime around 1840 it became customary for the well-to-do families of this and other geographical areas to enclose the breezeway, thus producing a "central passage house," the idea for which may indicate Georgian influence. A central passage house stacked atop another results in what scholars refer to as an "I-house," a form particularly common among the Upper Cumberland's more affluent families.

With the widespread availability of sawmills in the region by the 1820s, all these house forms could be constructed of either log or sawn board on frame (weatherboards). Planks soon covered most log structures. Weatherboarded log dwellings were very popular in the Upper Cumberland between the Civil War and 1900. After that, log building construction faded rapidly, although a few log pole barns were built as late as 1945 due mainly to tradition, low income levels, and abundant stands of native timber.

Colonial revival styles, along with one- and two-story bungalows, became popular at the beginning of the twentieth century and began to replace many of the older folk architectural forms. The ubiquitous ranch-style house was introduced in the 1950s, and new construction of these houses was common through the 1970s, at which time colonial revivals reappeared. The architectural landscape at the beginning of the 1990s thus contains an interesting blend of the older folk forms and the newer blueprint houses.

EARLY HOUSEHOLDS

Fire for domestic heating and cooking was a precious commodity for pre-1900 residents of the Upper Cumberland. G. H. Harbison of Hickory College, Metcalfe County, told how fire was obtained and of the efforts taken to prevent it from going out:

People used to save fire from breakfast 'til dinner and dinner 'til night in the fireplace in the summertime. They'd put it back in the corner and cover it with ashes to keep it from going out.

If they run out and they had to create a new fire, they would take and go to their neighbors and borrow fire. If it became necessary for them to create a fire on a hunting trip or on a long journey, they would take a little gunpowder and a little piece of tow; they would have a little piece of flint and steel and strike the steel against the flint and cause a spark to fly. It would set the gunpowder on fire and that would catch the tow and some dry kindling on fire.

With careful nurturing, they would get a fire going.

Hubert Branham of Albany described a man displaced by the construction of Wolf Creek Dam in the early 1940s whose fire had not been allowed to die out in over a century:

When Wolf Creek Dam was put in, they moved all the people out from the hills and hollows down there. There was one old fellow who had a fire in his fireplace that hadn't been out in over a hundred years.

He wouldn't leave it. So they took a big truck in there, tore the chimney down part way, put the fire and wood and a man to see to it on the truck. They took his fireplace out from there, fire and all, and put it back up for him [at the new location].

He would have [stubbornly remained with the house and] drowned when the house was covered by water if they had put his fire out.

The Reverend A. B. Wright, an early Methodist circuit rider, wrote of life in northern Fentress County shortly after that area was populated:

I was born [1826] just thirty years after Tennessee became a state, and before there were any railroads or telegraph lines. . . . The mode of living was primitive. The people of the rural parts lived in log houses. A cook-stove was an unknown luxury. People cut their small grain with a reap-hook, and thrashed it by trampling it out with horses. Wild animals were abundant. Many a night have I heard the wolves howl about our home. Deer were plentiful, and wild bears were not unusual. Wild turkeys were to be found in large flocks. . . . People used the products of their own hands both for food and for clothing, there being very few manufactured goods of any kind.

Household furnishings differed in accordance with the size and financial status of the individual families. Tom Garland of Burnside, born in 1904, described the home of his youth.

We were a large family with two large rooms and fireplaces in each room, and a lean-to kitchen and dining room built on. We also had an unfinished attic with a tin roof showing through the strips. The stairs that went up to it were very steep and very difficult to negotiate.

We had four beds in the attic, and that's where the boys slept. There were cracks where the chimney went through the roof. Many cold mornings, I've shook a fine powder of snow off the bedcovers when I got up.

My mother used to put her smoothing irons in front of the fireplace near the open coal grate and get them hot. She would then wrap them in a towel and take them into the attic and put them at the foot of the bed to have a warm place to place our cold feet when we went to bed.

I remember my father sitting in front of the fireplace with his cobbler's outfit putting half soles on our shoes so we could go to school the next day.

The quality and abundance of household furnishings were as varied as the families that populated the Upper Cumberland area. Cumberland County resident J. W. Wells of Burkesville, whose childhood home in the Irish Bottom community exemplified the more affluent level of rural society, described what his family's household furnishings were like in the late nineteenth century:

It took several beds to supply the family. The steads were made of choicest cherry and walnut timbers fashioned by the turning-lathe which wrought the bed posts into the most fancy designs of carvings of knobs, triangles, cylinders, and fancy heads with beautiful carved rounds. The steads were made to stand high from the floor, giving room for the tiny trundles to stand beneath them in daytime. Every bed was furnished with the choicest homemade quilts and blankets, overspreading fat featherbeds on both large and small, made of feathers picked from the sixty or more head of geese that were always kept. The bed dressings were supported not on slats, but on ropes made of the hemp grown in fields. . . . Floors were kept clean with brooms that were home-tied, and also with the family mops made by boring a six- by twelve-inch poplar plank full of holes into which were inserted twisted shucks from the cribs.

Chairs were made of sugar tree for the posts and rounds, and hickory bark, cut in long one-inch strips from young hickories and platted, was used for the bottoms which lasted for many years. . . . Other articles found in the kitchen were the cedar churn, cedar water buckets, milk piggins, buckeye tray, coffee mill, sieves, meal barrel, pot rack and salt gourd.

From a less affluent family perhaps, Bea Pitman of southern Clinton County recalled the two wood-burning stoves in her home when she was a young girl:

I learned to cook when I was five years old. I had to stand up in a little chair to reach the stove. We had an old step-stove. . . .

We lived on the hill in a little log cabin. We had an old heating stove down in a box of mud. Well, it caught afire when I was six years old. I took ahold of it, but couldn't move the stove by myself. So I threw water in the stove and put the fire out inside the stove. But it still burnt a hole through the mud and caught the floor on fire.

Until recent years, most of the houses occupied by people of the Upper Cumberland were essentially small in size. Of the 121 homes in Jackson County visited by Walter B. Overton in the mid-1920s, twenty-

This stone spring house once served the water and refrigeration needs of two northern Monroe county families. (Photo by the author)

four had four rooms, thirty-eight had three, twenty-three had two, and two of the houses were of the single-pen variety. Only two homes had running water—provided by elevated tanks that caught and held rainwater. Five houses were equipped with cisterns, and in seventy-four water was obtained from nearby wells; residents in the remaining homes were required to carry their water from springs. Only one-third of the structures Overton visited were painted at the time, but almost one-half of them were equipped with telephones.

The typical farm home during most of the nineteenth century and the first thirty years of the twentieth had only the necessary furnishings, with few frills included. Since none of these homes had indoor bath facilities, privacy was at a premium. Family members and guests alike went outside "to count the stars" before retiring for the night. Guests often slept in the host family's living room or the smaller children's bedroom.

"Some people of today might question the modesty of such arrangements," writes C. L. Holt, Overton County itinerant Methodist minister, "but when the time came to retire, lights were extinguished and the room was in total darkness. In homes with more than one bedroom, modesty was enhanced by assigning men and boys to one room, and the females to another." Larger homes had parlors that were seldom used except for company. The parlor often contained a bed for guests, a large dresser or bureau, and a pump organ.

Small children of the same gender often slept in a bed in the room with their parents. At other times, the father and a small son slept in one bed while the mother and a small daughter slept in another bed in the same room. The husband and wife had to wait until the children were asleep before they could enjoy private times together. Three elderly women, my mother included, told of times when the parents thought the kids were asleep but weren't! I asked one woman from southern Wayne County, who had numerous siblings, how her parents ever found enough private time to have that many children.

"Hump-h-h," she jokingly retorted, "the older kids had to go to school, didn't they!"

EARLY SELF-SUFFICIENCY

Rich or poor, families across the region used lye soap on laundry days throughout the first three decades of the twentieth century. Until around 1915, in the early spring people made soap at home using lye leached from wood ashes poured into an ash hopper. This process, which involved putting raw meat scraps into a kettle of boiling lye water, was generally done at the time of the waning of the moon to prevent the substance from boiling over too frequently. The meat was cooked until it liquified, thus providing the grease necessary to produce the soap.

"Later on, people used commercial lye that made a hard brown soap, which we used for years," writes Lynnie White of Monticello. "This was a good soap and really lathered. Back then, there were no detergents, no bleach, just soap. If our clothes needed bleaching, we put some peach tree leaves or gimpsonweed [*sic*] leaves in a flour sack, tied it up, and put it in the kettle where the clothes were boiling. This whitened the clothes."

Landon Anderson of Celina remembered the days when people took their dirty clothes to a creek or to the Cumberland River:

They'd take a steer and drag their pots that didn't have legs on them down to the stream. There, they'd wash their clothes and beat them out on a big rock. Later on, they got these grooved washboards.

My sister helped Mother wash until she got married, and then it fell my place. Well, Mother wouldn't allow anything to be washed out on the washboards but her sheets, pillow cases, bolster slips, and shirts. When it come to overalls, she'd yell, "No, you can't wash them on there! Them old buttons will tear my rub board all to pieces."

Women and children employed battling sticks (long paddles resembling oars) to beat the dirt out of work clothes after they had been adequately soaked in lye-soap water. When all the garments had been washed and rinsed in a tub of clear, cold water, they were wrung out and hung on a clothesline to dry in the sun. It took two people to lift and wring out the large, heavy items such as quilts, blankets, and bedspreads.

Upper Cumberland people of earlier times were totally dependent on the presence of free-flowing, perennial fresh water pouring from caves, bluffs, and bubbling springs. Lucky indeed were those people who found both spring and creek water on their new landholdings. Together these two sources of water could fill every need for family drinking water, sanitation, and livestock consumption.

The water table in the Upper Cumberland of pioneer times was closer to the surface of the land than it is today. Oral testimonies from area residents describe one-time surface streams that have vanished during the last two-thirds of the twentieth century because of the lowered water table caused by the ravages of human-induced erosion of the watersheds. Existent rock walls around former spring sites stand as mute testimony to a way of life that flourished between 1800 and the 1930s. The same is true for dried-up, hand-dug wells lined with hewn stones, some of which were capped and sealed over to accommodate metal hand pumps. During that period of time, these freshwater springs and dug wells served as the only means of refrigerating food, according to Oral Page of Tompkins-ville:

I remember when people would carry milk and butter and put it in the spring. I remember that my aunt had a big spring where there was a big, flat rock. And somebody took a hammer and coal chisel and just chiselled out holes in that big rock.

The holes were of various sizes. Some would fit buckets, and some would fit dishes and jars. They'd just set their milk and butter and stuff there in that water that was running out of the spring, just ice cold. That was the coldest water I ever drank in my life not to have ice in it.

And I remember that when we'd come in from the field for dinner [lunch], my job was always to go to the spring and get the milk and butter. I remember one time I went down to get it and some fox hounds had turned the bucket of milk over and had eaten the bowl of butter, and so I came back to the house without either.

Octogenarian James Frank Butler of Cumberland County, Kentucky, acknowledged the obvious, that milk refrigerated in springs or wells did occasionally "blink [spoil] or clabber." "You'd drink it just the same," Butler said. "The old people just done the best they could."

Almost without exception, dowsers were used to "witch" wells dug in the region before the 1930s. A dowser, or water witch, is a person perceived to have a skill for discovering underground water with the use of a divining rod, usually a small, forked limb cut from virtually any fruit-bearing tree or willow. Because a water witch's method is not scientifically proven, reliance on this technique is considered a folk practice. However, there were at least 25,000 active diviners in the United States as late as the mid-1950s, according to folklorist Trudy Balcom, and the results of their predictions have proven as successful as those of hydrologists and geologists.

Dowsers were often called in before a new home was built, so that the house could be located near a well. To find the water, the dowser typically holds the free ends of the forked prongs, wrists turned upward. Thumbs are pointed horizontally outwards so that the loose ends of the prongs extend three to four inches beyond the thumbs. (There are variations on the manner in which the switch is held.) The dowser walks slowly toward the desired location of the well. When the witch comes upon a subterranean stream immediately below, the vertex of the fork turns toward the ground; the stronger the stream, the more forceful the downward pull. The fork often twists in the dowser's hands when a strong stream of water is discovered. Some say that the bark will even twist off into the dowser's hands, and a few people claim that the forked limb often begins to nod, one time for each foot of dirt and rock that will have to be excavated before water is reached. Once the water has been witched, it is necessary to bring in a person skilled at excavating dirt and loose rock and lining the walls of the well shaft with stones so as to prevent future cave-ins, thus ensuring a dependable supply of water.

A BARTER ECONOMY

A family's ability to be self-sufficient was the key factor to survival before World War II. Whether gathered, hunted, or raised agriculturally, the food supply of this traditional culture depended on what the natural environment provided. People either grew what they ate or extracted it from nature's abundant storehouse in the form of wild meat, greens, nuts, herbs, and fruits.

James Frank Butler recalled how people acquired the basic necessities at the beginning of the twentieth century:

You spent money only on things that you couldn't raise at home—salt, sugar, things like that.

Made your own meat at home. If you didn't, you didn't have any unless you bought it from a neighbor. Sometimes you'd take things to the store to trade for other things that you had to have, like clothing.

My mother picked her geese every five weeks and sold them feathers.

Brought forty-five cents a pound. She had forty-five or fifty geese that she'd pick the feathers from. Took four geese to make a pound. And she'd take them feathers to the store and she'd come back with the awfulest load of stuff you ever seen.

Kenneth Irvin of Creelsboro, a river village in Russell County, recalled that numerous people in that area brought poultry, beeswax, ginseng, and dried apples from home to use in the bartering process at his father's store. These same items, among others, were used elsewhere across the region as the basis for trades negotiated at the community general store—that venerated institution that once served as the meeting-place of the Upper Cumberland. Adele Mitchell of Edmonton, explaining that her family had no cash just before World War I, described the process of trading chickens for Easter bonnets at the general store:

Easter was a very special day around Wisdom. That's when we'd always get our Easter bonnet. We raised a crop of chickens early in the spring to trade for our bonnets. And we usually walked and carried the chickens by hand in baskets. The funny thing about it was that the chickens would never offer to move around on the way there. But just the minute you got to the store and set your basket down on the scales, they were sure to start flopping. And you'd have to chase them to get them back in. That was so embarrassing!

One is reminded here of the apocryphal story told in and around White County about the fellow who took a rooster to the store to trade for some tobacco. The merchant weighed the rooster, then instructed the customer to go around behind the store and put it in the pen with the other chickens. After stealing the bird from the merchant's pen, a second fellow walked through the front door of the store and handed it to the merchant to be weighed. The merchant noticed the similarity between the two roosters but said nothing. He weighed the rooster, then instructed the man to place it in the pen with the others. When still a third thief walked into the store with the rooster in hand, the merchant, perhaps aware of the man's financial plight, said, "I already know what it weighs, just take it around back and put it in there with the others."

As in other areas of rural and small-town America, legal tender was scarce in the Upper Cumberland, and barter was the main means of exchange. It was not until after industrialization caused a boom in bank construction near the end of the nineteenth century that the buying and selling of goods on a product-for-product basis increased appreciably.

As indicated, the leaders of this barter economy were the local merchants who willingly exchanged retail commodities for surplus agricultural products, animal hides, and dried medicinal roots such as ginseng and yellowroot. The following account given by Landon Anderson of Celina indicates that area merchants often bartered for certain less-than-desirable items:

> On the ridge west of here, chestnuts were a big thing. They'd gather all they could eat, then take the rest of them and sell them. I was at Barris's store once, and no telling how many bushels of chestnuts he had there. And worms was all over the floor, crawling out on the store porch.

After selecting commodities, customers who had nothing to barter were often heard to say, "Put that on the books; I'll pay you when I sell my tobacco this fall." Most of them did, as people of that era still lived comfortably with the saying, "My word is my honor." Some did not honor their word, however, and some store proprietors eventually had to close their doors. One customer in the Mt. Gilead section of Monroe County owed the owner $4,200 when the store closed down in the late 1930s.

Grist and roller mill operators in the community provided services on a similar basis. They ground corn and wheat in exchange for a "toll," that is, a standard portion of the meal or flour itself. Historian Ron Eller writes, "This form of commerce reinforced the autonomy of the local market system and provided [local] communities with considerable freedom from the fluctuations of the national cash economy."

Since farm owners had little or no cash, they frequently paid their hired laborers with meat or corn. John Stone of eastern Cumberland County, Kentucky, recalled that his father-in-law generally butchered fifteen hogs each year, knowing that some of the meat would be given to his workers. In such instances, the farm owner and the laborer came to a pre-work agreement of so many pounds of meat or corn for a day's work. A bushel of shelled corn suitable for grinding into meal or four to five pounds of meat was a fairly standard wage.

Arnold Watson, resident of the Kettle community in that same county, remembered that during the late 1800s his father paid about twenty-five cents for a week's labor in the fields. And as late as the 1930s in my home community of Rock Bridge, Monroe County, standard farm wages for a day's work had risen to only fifty cents, plus lunch.

Dave Wright of western Fentress County, who lived and farmed in the tradition of his ancestors until 1948, epitomizes the self-sufficient farmer of recent times. I first met Dave Wright in 1972 when I stopped to ask for directions to the Indian Creek vicinity of western Fentress. Not hearing my question, or intentionally ignoring it, Wright, who was then ninety-two years old, looked wistfully at the tall mountain-like knob located about one mile behind his house.

"Mister, do you see that mountain?" he wanted to know. Without waiting for my response, he continued, "Well, mister, I own that mountain." Appropriately enough, it is named Wright Mountain.

The old Wright homeplace was located near the top of the mountain, and I was permitted to go see it firsthand. Still standing was a deserted single-pen log cabin with a kitchen lean-to, an attic for sleeping, and a moonshine still in the cellar. Weeds and tall bushes engulfed the cabin, but hollyhocks and rose bushes remained in evidence in the front yard. Twenty feet behind the cabin stood the smokehouse. Adjacent to it was an old garden site and the spot where the Wrights had kept thirty-five beehives and gums.

The Wright farm had at one time contained a thriving orchard, attested to by rotted trunks and stumps of apple trees. A cave spring located two hundred feet farther up the side of the mountain had provided continuous water for the house and livestock by means of a U-shaped wooden flume carved from tree saplings. Also in evidence were a hog house, a combination corn crib-tool shed, and a double crib barn, all of log construction. Next to the barn was a small cornfield; other small fields, often referred to as patches, were some distance away. The Dave Wright family, comprising six members, had procured meat by hunting wild animals and butchering domesticated raw-boned hogs. Wright commented that he could "step out the back door any time and kill five or six squirrels." Fruits and vegetables came from the orchard and garden; sweets consisted of honey, molasses, maple syrup and, on occasion, sugar purchased at a distant general store.

When I met them, Dave Wright and his wife were living at the foot of the mountain on Big Indian Creek in a modest four-room house. They had built the house on acreage purchased in 1948, three years after their son Stanley returned home from the war, carrying a battery-powered radio set under his arm. Before that, they had never heard a radio broadcast.

I learned that Dave Wright had not been "back home" up on the mountain for many years, since the place was hard to reach except on foot. The body of the last person to die there, in a spot more remote than the Wrights', had to be carried off the mountain on the shoulders of four men. I asked Wright to compare his present life-style with his earlier days on the mountain. His response was couched in remorse. "Mister, the day I left the mountain," he said, "that's the day I unwrapped the candy bar." For him, life had dried out and turned stale.

Low-income, self-sufficient families were also found in the coal-bearing portions of Cumberland Mountain on both sides of the state line. Bee Wallace of Monticello described the small family-centered mining operations that he could remember. "Children would help their parents haul it out of the mines in wheelbarrows," he recalled. "They sold it for forty cents a ton during the Depression years, or bartered it at stores for flour, meal, meat, and just about anything else in the line of food."

Every family and community across the Upper Cumberland from pioneer times through the Great Depression years of the 1930s practiced bartering in the form of shared labor. Work-time activities in those days often took the form of social recreation as well. Women working on a quilt together would be provided an opportunity for female bonding as well as producing a much-needed product. In earlier times, the older women present customarily cooked while the younger ones quilted. After the meal, everyone worked as a team to finish the project.

Mixed-gender activities such as corn huskings, bean and pea shellings, and apple peelings were commonplace. Wheat threshings, log rollings, and house raisings were primarily left to the men. But whatever the job, such activities were clarion calls to members of the community to gather for work that also served as play.

These get-togethers were cause for the preparation of huge meals. Women cooked and served all manner of food, including gingerbread and cookies, along with cider and other homemade beverages (homebrew at times), if the occasion lasted until the evening hours. In 1976 I happened upon a communal effort by a group of men in Buffalo Cove, Tennessee, to repair a church building. When lunchtime arrived, women of the church brought prepared dishes and served their working husbands a wholesome meal, which was accompanied by hearty laughter and good-natured fellowship.

DOMESTIC INDUSTRIES

In addition to farming, the sharing of work, and the hunting-fishing-gathering activities (including pearling along the Cumberland) that were common to all pre-industrial societies, domestic industries designed to serve family needs also made self-sufficiency possible. Homes were the first centers of industry in the Upper Cumberland. Throughout the year, families actively engaged in yarn spinning, dyeing, weaving, carding cotton, quilting, making leather boots and shoes, canning and/or burying fruits and vegetables for consumption during winter months, making handtools for use around the house and farm, and blacksmithing.

Will Jones of Leslie, Cumberland County, Kentucky, recalled how at the turn of the century, his mother made each of her children two pairs of stockings from spun yarn. "We had to wear them all the time until spring of the year, when they let us go barefooted," Jones reminisced. In efforts to speed up the coming of spring, he said, "We would run and

scrub the bottoms out as soon as we could, for when the bottoms wore out, she would let us pull them off."

Quilting is a folk craft—some would say art—that was known and practiced by free women and slaves, rich and poor alike, from pioneer times to the present. Early quilts made in the Upper Cumberland, as elsewhere, involved two different stages of needlework. The "patch-work" process called for the sewing together of various patches or pieces of material, while "quilting" involved the fastening together of two layers of cloth with a layer of carded-cotton filler in between.

Throughout the years of self-sufficiency in the Upper Cumberland, women's magazines and farm journals reproduced quilt patterns and often provided suggestions for fabric, print, and color. Thus it was that local women learned about patterns such as the Flower Garden, Log Cabin, Double Wedding Ring, Crazy, Album, Friendship, Dresden Plate, and numerous others.

A household in southern Cumberland County, Kentucky, 1972 (Photo by David Sutherland)

Jewell Thomas of Burkesville wrote of the time her maternal grandmother taught her to make a Sunshine and Shade quilt:

My grandmother was a marvelous little lady. When I was very young, she always seemed to be very old. My first memories of her are as a grey haired little woman, with her hair pulled back into a bun, either on top of her head or at the nape of her neck.

In the wintertime she spent hours and hours cutting small pieces of material into even smaller pieces to form a pattern. The patterns were then pieced into blocks and set together with matching solids or the blocks themselves set together one against another until a bed size quilt was formed.

She always did her own quilting and could make some of the smallest stitches I have ever seen.

When she had cut out pieces for her pieced blocks she carefully kept the strings so that they could be pieced into string quilts. Numerous patterns were used; I remember she had a "Sunshine and Shade" and several made up of pieced stars. I was fascinated with watching her piece quilts and kept begging that I be allowed to do one of my own. I believe that I was about eight years old when she promised me that we would work on a quilt for me. She would teach me how to piece a quilt!

She helped me get the Sears and Roebuck catalog and cut several dozen diamonds. The idea of the paper was that it was the basic pattern. When the pieces of materials were sewn together they were stitched through the paper diamond. The edges were then trimmed to form a star. To complete the pattern of the quilt eight of the stars were sewn together; after that the paper pattern was carefully torn away.

Every spare minute was spent at my grandmother's home because I was working on MY QUILT.

I remember the winter was very cold and the only heat in my grandmother's living room was from a great big fireplace....

There were no electric lights in the house but there were two very good coal oil lamps that we always used. The nook in which we pieced the quilt had two windows that reached to within 18 inches of the floor, and if the day wasn't extremely dark, we used the natural light in which to work.

The first block that I put together was an absolute delight.... My stitches were not too neat nor small, but my effort was constantly praised and gently urged to make them just a little smaller or just take a little more time to do them....

My quilt was completed before spring because she would help me when I reached a point of discouragement. She then helped me card home grown cotton for a filler for the quilt. My grandfather's sister was called upon to do the quilting and she did a beautiful job.

I still have the quilt! I used it while I was growing up, I have used it to cover my children and now it is tattered and torn, but I could never part with the quilt. It has a tremendous amount of love sewn into each string diamond.

Quilting became less common everywhere in the years after World War II. By the 1970s, however, a resurgence of interest in this artistic craft form swept across the Upper Cumberland. Today, quilting guilds located in Cookeville, Crossville, Gainesboro, and Sparta are actively involved in rejuvenating this traditional practice. Nowadays the tops are often made on a sewing machine, but the actual quilting is still done by the hands of guild members who sit in a group around the work.

Many people in the region had home industries involving tanyards, leather-tanning procedures, and shoemaking. In the tanning process, animal hides would be encased in tree bark and buried underground, where the bundle would remain for ten to twelve months until spring. In the meantime, if the hides were to be used for shoes, the cobbler would have whittled out shoe pegs from maple wood to be used, when seasoned, in fastening the soles of the boots and shoes to their upper portions.

In early times, tanned hides not used in the home community for making shoes, saddles, and harness were placed on flatboats and shipped to Nashville and New Orleans. Cobblers and saddle-and-harness makers used the bulk of the hides at home, however, as their skilled services were in great demand, especially before the Civil War.

Thongs, shoelaces, and other leather items came from the hides of buffalo, hog, deer, bear, and groundhog. Groundhogs especially served two basic purposes. "They'd take that groundhog hide and stretch it on a board and let it dry out and then they would make shoe strings," observed Lena Howell Martin of Gainesboro.

"And they made the best banjo heads in the country," added Landon Anderson of Celina.

Hides tanned with the fur on them were used for rugs, robes, coverlets, and upholstery. The hides of buffalo and bear were especially popular for these purposes.

Most early farmers did much of their own shoeing of horses, sharpening of plow points, and otherwise making out as best they could with their own bellows, anvils, and handtools. The coming of a blacksmith into the community was a real blessing. He was a master of all trades, performing skilled jobs such as shoeing horses, welding iron, and repairing furniture. The charcoal used in the forge was a semi-powdered, strong-smelling substance that produced a heavy smoke. Just as the livery stable and smokehouse had their own distinctive odors, so, too, did the blacksmith shop, and no one seemed to mind the smell of horses' hoofs seared by still-hot metal shoes.

Ostensibly the fellows gathered at the shop had come on business, but no one would urge the blacksmith to hurry up with his job. This was a folk event in the true sense of the word. The shop served the same social function as the general store, providing men with a place to loaf and indulge in leisurely conversation.

One or more members of each family performed virtually all craft activities at home. Items they made and the tools they used in the various processes were functional adjuncts to the house and farm. People today gleefully pounce upon these artifacts because of their delicate lines, balance, symmetry, and fine texture. Originally, however, the items were prized because they served daily needs. Functional considerations overrode the aesthetic dimension, which is not always the case with the arts and crafts items made by some of today's practitioners.

By the early 1930s, virtually every community in the Upper Cumberland, and many individual families as well, enjoyed the services of one or more of these craftspersons. They whittled small objects from wood, made flint marbles, carved out ax and hammer handles and scraped them with pieces of broken glass until they were perfectly smooth, built boats for use at the river crossings, and made caskets for the community's deceased.

Folklorist Roby Cogswell observes that while most people nowadays use traditional handmade objects to decorate their homes, the Upper Cumberland region serves to remind us that the nostalgic symbolism of folk craftwork reflects real and tangible connections to traditional ways of life in the not-too-distant past. In certain sections of neighboring Southern Appalachia, much attention has been paid to the folk arts and crafts traditions. At the same time, the Upper Cumberland has unconsciously nurtured a rather distinctive and expressive folk culture—one that remains vibrant in the early 1990s and sends forth both tangible and intangible reminders that people here are linked together because of their shared past and an inherited sense of place. Traditional arts and crafts have been and still are an integral part of Upper Cumberland folklife. The numerous baskets, chairs, quilts, pieces of furniture, and wood carvings made here that have gone to other places around the country embody their makers' generational skills and regional traditions.

There have been losses along the way. One was a leading pottery area in Tennessee on the western edge of the Cumberland Plateau in DeKalb, White, and Putnam counties, where fine local clays were used in important stoneware centers by the 1820s. Over the years, dozens of potteries, many associated with generations of the LaFever, Hedgecough, Roberts, and Dunn families, made functional salt-glazed ware for a regional market. They used the horse-powered pug mills, kick-wheels, and wood-fired kilns that characterized the old-time potter's technology.

Some of that technology changed over time, but with competition from glass and other container materials, handmade pottery gradually became obsolete. With the closing of the Cookeville Pottery in 1961, the last traditional pottery ceased operation. Today, only school-trained potters work in the Upper Cumberland. In recent years, however, the antique market has rediscovered old locally crafted pitchers, churns, and jars characterized by graceful shapes and distinctive dusky brown and green tones.

Just as natural clay deposits spawned potteries, the Upper Cumberland's greatest natural resource—timber—afforded materials for numerous traditional handskills in the region. Timber, along with farming, was central to the area's economic well-being in earlier times. The harvesting of huge trees, often floated or rafted downstream from remote sections of the Upper Cumberland, afforded many families their chief source of cash income and contact with the outside world. The presence of these forests fostered an intimate familiarity with different woods, their properties and uses, and with woodworking tools and techniques.

Even as times changed, woodcrafting skills were passed along to subsequent generations. For example, hewing logs with a broadax, essential in the building of early barns and houses, remained relevant to current needs long after newer kinds of construction took over. Woodsmen still hacked railroad ties by hand in some places as late as the 1940s. Long after roofs of tin and asphalt became common, the technique once used to make board shingles—"riving" wood with a froe and mallet—remained the preferred method for producing high-quality hickory and oak tobacco sticks used in the harvesting of burley. The adoption of efficient power tools and increased mechanization evident in countless small sawmills presently operating across the Upper Cumberland has surely influenced the kinds of folk skills currently practiced. But the resultant changes have been gradual, blending the old with the new in the toolboxes and talents of area woodworkers.

The kinds of occupations associated with timber illustrate continuities between handcrafts and more mechanized production in the evolution of industries important to the region's economy. While we normally associate folk craft activities with households and small shops, this sort of work can play an important role in molding large-scale businesses as well. The commercial production of tool handles is a good example. At one time, self-sufficient farmers and timberworkers routinely carved their own handles of all types using a drawknife and shaving horse. Skilled handlemakers sometimes became specialist craftsmen, and their small shops grew into factories producing handles for sale on the commercial market. Power machinery replaced woodcarving, and the manufacturing endeavors of Turner, Day, and Woolworth Handle Corporation in Crossville, the Sparta Spoke Factory, Cookeville Handle Company, and similar establishments across the region superseded domestic handcrafting of wood items.

The process of mechanization and growth is not just a recent one. Mills using the region's abundant water power even in early days sought to increase the scale and speed of traditional craftwork. Asa Faulkner began weaving coverlets and the like with his water-powered looms in Warren County in the early 1800s, and over the next century the operation expanded into the extensive Tennessee Woolen Mills Plant. The many firms associated with the beautiful pink-tinged Crab Orchard stone distinctive to Cumberland County, Tennessee, continue to rely on forms of traditional handwork in quarrying and rock masonry.

Once finished, surplus handmade items were traded within the community or taken to the county seat towns and sold there for small amounts of cash. The February 15, 1938, issue of *The Tompkinsville News* noted that local broommaker C. L. Tooley had made more than two thousand brooms during the previous five months. In Pickett County, Si Pearce of the Williams Chapel community and Louis Thomas of Chanute, like their counterparts across the region, made white oak baskets for their neighbors before and during the Depression. As payment for each basket, they asked that it be filled with shelled corn. Open-market sales of Upper Cumberland craft items increased dramatically following World War I, and roadside stands became commonplace during the 1920s and 1930s.

Chair shops across the region, now more mechanized than in former years, turn local oak and other hardwoods into sturdy ladderbacks. Notable ladderback chairmakers in Kentucky include Frank and Willie Burley, residents of the Cherry Tree Ridge section of southern Cumberland County. Some Tennessee chairmakers are the Doss family of near Jamestown, who still have a foot-powered springpole lathe in operation; Sam Sewell of Lafayette; the Tabors of near Crossville, known for their excellent quality "settin'" chairs since 1806; and the Hicks family from Chanute, Pickett County. Quinn Davidson of Chanute claimed that John Hicks, his son Hague, and Hague's son John had been involved with chairmaking for as long as he could remember. Davidson was sitting in a Hague Hicks platform rocker at the time I talked with him. "Hague made this one in 1912," he told me. "I know, 'cause it was set down in the diary book when Mom bought it. I remember as a kid seeing him bring it here. Soon as he left, we all piled on it!" The Hicks family closed shop a few years later with the premature death of young John.

Sixty or so miles to the west in the Jennings Creek area of southeastern Macon County, another Hicks, Amos (c. 1900–1980), married Bessy Newberry, who was a sister of Andrew and Dallas Newberry (1892–

In eastern Macon County, Louis Newberry, foreground, and his two sons represent the fourth and fifth generations of family chairmakers. (Photo by the author)

1990), both old-time chairmakers. Amos, not a chairmaker by trade, soon picked it up from his brothers-in-law and worked for many years in partnership with Dallas. Their wives skillfully wove the chair bottoms with strips of bark taken from hickory trees.

Andrew and Dallas Newberry learned how to make chairs from their father, Lewis Tolbert (Tol) Newberry (1860–1919), who had picked up the skills of the trade from his father, Billy Newberry (1824–1900). Today, Dallas's son, Louis, who was born in 1943, and Louis's two sons, Terry and Mark, both in their twenties, are following in the footsteps of their forebears.

These craftsmen begin by cutting the trees on their farm woodlots. The desired tree—cherry, walnut, maple, ash, or oak—is cut into lengths for chair posts. The cuts are permitted to dry out (season) and are split with a sledge and wedge. The wood for the posts is then ready for the handmade lathe, which is powered by a used appliance motor rather than a foot treadle such as the one used by the older Newberrys.

The back and chair rounds are seasoned in a smoke chamber over burning shavings and then driven into the chair post. As the chair timbers continue to season, the greener posts tighten naturally and grip the back and rounds. Nails are not used. The person who placed the order, whether for one chair or a truckload, picks up the finished product at the shop. The Newberrys have no production manager or sales agent.

Terry and Mark represent the fifth generation of Newberrys involved in chairmaking. When I asked them what would happen to the family craft business in the event of their father's premature death, Terry responded, "Keep making chairs, I guess. It's been going on for five generations, so there ain't no use in stopping now."

Craftspeople such as the Newberrys learned their traditional skills through rigorous but informal on-the-job training. Just as the proprietor of a general store on a lunch break might instruct his son or daughter to go sell a pound of coffee to a customer only after he or she had been taught the procedure, a chairmaker's son was never told to turn a chair leg on a lathe before he had been guided through the process several times.

The Haile brothers of Monroe County, Kentucky, were familiar with the practice of family apprenticeships. Hascal Haile of Tompkinsville and his brother, Thomas Vose Haile of Louisville, were two of the most artistic woodworkers ever to reside in the Upper Cumberland. They were born in 1906 and 1910 to a family of traditional carpenters and cabinet-makers. Their great-grandfather made caskets for the community before and during the Civil War; their grandfather, Dr. Thomas Haile, was a country "saddlebag" physician and also a skilled woodworker; and their father John Haile was a farmer-cabinetmaker. All three lived and died on the banks of the Cumberland River in the Vernon community where Hack and Tom were also born.

The two brothers spent their early years making every wooden item conceivable, from large logging wagons to caskets. Hack recalled making more than thirty-five caskets during the flux epidemic of 1934. (Flux was a violent intestinal disorder that killed hundreds of local residents.) As did all area casketmakers, the brothers donated the yellow poplar con-tainers to the victims' families. With their father, Hack and Tom made skiffs, johnboats, and other craft for their neighbors and the various crosstie companies that operated along the river.

The two Haile brothers moved to Tompkinsville, their county seat, and opened a furniture shop in 1936. Tom moved on to Louisville in 1940 and worked there for Shackleford's music store for many years before turning his full attention to making and repairing violins, cellos, and banjos, specializing in classical models. He served as an apprentice for the Del'Proto family of European violin makers and was acclaimed as America's leading Stradivarius repairman from the 1950s through the 1970s.

Hascal Haile continued on in Tompkinsville where he earned a comfortable living making some of the finest pieces of handcrafted furniture and cabinets produced anywhere. During the 1950s, he began making grandfather clock frames from native cherry and walnut timber, some of which had been sawn back in 1868. His pieces are now all collectors' items.

Hack began making guitars for professional musicians in 1960. He had made them as a hobby since he was twelve years old. "In those early days," Haile recalled, "if you didn't make them yourself, you didn't have any toys or musical instruments at all. Everything we got commercially came in by steamboat; there weren't any highways back then." Hack remembered that in making their first banjo, he and Tom stole one of their mother's cake pans and used it in making a pot for the banjo. Then they robbed a hen's nest and sold the eggs to buy cheap strings that were shipped in by boat.

Musicians such as Bobby Goldsboro, Hank Snow, Dolly Parton, Jerry Reed, and Chet Atkins use Haile guitars, and the Smithsonian Institution requested the Haile guitar that Atkins was using when he won the Grammy Award for guitar finesse. It was Atkins who first tested and endorsed Haile's classical guitars, reputedly the most complicated instruments in the world to make. Leading musicians from Europe and America kept Haile's supply of classical and folk guitars bought up.

Haile learned the basics of his craft in the traditional manner, following those procedures for many years. The fact that he used power tools in later years to expedite his work did not diminish his role as a folk craftsman. Deploring mass production, Hascal Haile continued throughout his active years to assemble his guitars by hand.

Another gifted woodworker was Clarence Hawkins of Red Boiling Springs, Tennessee, who won regional and national acclaim for the high-quality items of furniture handcrafted in his small shop at the edge of town during the second and third quarters of the twentieth century. He worked with native woods, including wild red cherry, black walnut, and curly maple. The furniture was finished in the natural colors of the wood.

Hawkins began his furniture-making operation in the days when it was still common to use a small lathe turned by a footpowered treadle. He eventually secured a motor from a used automobile and geared up a mechanical rig to turn the lathe; in later years, he used electricity. The remainder of his work was done by hand in accordance with time-tested procedures. He made chair posts from unseasoned wood and the rounds from seasoned timber; the bottoms were fashioned from hickory bark or corn shucks. Hawkins boasted that a finished chair was "as steady as a rock and as solid as a jug."

Throughout the Upper Cumberland, folk crafts continue to connect the past and the present. In most parts of this forest-covered region, older people recall when handmade baskets, chairs, quilts, beds, tables, chests, handles, plates, spoons, bowls, rolling pins, dough trays, washstands, barrels, and kegs were a real part of everyday life. Virtually every community has collective memories of the gifted people who made these products, which still grace homes and business establishments. Many of the craftspeople are deceased or have been inactive for more than half a century, but memories of them remain strong in the minds of surviving friends and relatives. The artifacts and the stories of their makers are an indelible presence.

The Family in Community Perspective

Song lyrics about mama, daddy, a dying brother or sister, a childhood sweetheart, the old homeplace, and other sentimental topics evoke nostalgic recollections of childhood for many who grew up in the Upper Cumberland. In spite of such strong memories, though, articulating the region's concept of family is not easy. Many generalizations about southern families have been made but few accounts of common folk experiences surrounding family life have been recorded.

Scholars here as elsewhere have not adequately addressed the images and structure of this venerated social unit. In the South, studies of family have focused primarily on antebellum life or, more recently, on Southern Appalachia. Certain information in these studies is relevant to the Upper Cumberland, but little has been written that is very useful for the present description of family folklife.

There is an extremely strong and lasting sense of identification with one's family group in this region. Part of this sense of belonging has to do with ownership of property, as land was and still is passed along from one generation to the next as a matter of course. Items of material culture and family memorabilia such as photos, furniture, pieces of clothing, hand tools, diaries, and newspapers bearing significant headlines allow younger family members to possess a part of the past in tangible form. Sometimes the giving and receiving of a family heirloom is transacted as a custom. For example, an ancestral brooch may be passed on to the family's first daughter to be married, or the great-grandfather's Civil War saddlebag becomes the inheritance of the eldest son.

There is a strong sense of mutual support among family members in the region, even through the maze of extended family ties. John Demos's description of the New England pre-modern family as "commonwealth" was applicable in the Upper Cumberland well into the twentieth century. Here, where members of an extended family remain in close contact through frequent visits, reunions, Memorial Day ceremonies, and church homecomings, it is still appropriate to view the community and family as concomitants. Many community residents are related, either closely or distantly.

Strong family ties in the region may be attributed to an agrarian social structure that has persisted across the years—a social matrix that is complemented by conservative religious thought and practices. In the day-to-day lives of Upper Cumberland people, religious strictures do not appear to define family dynamics, although it seems to be true that family order was and is influenced by evangelism, thus indicating a religious orientation. Unlike the Puritans who viewed children as evidence of human sin and demanded a child's accountability to God, southerners in general and Upper Cumberlanders in particular raised children with a more secular attitude. In this regard, Steven Stowe writes in *The Encyclopedia of Southern Culture* that "southern children were undisciplined compared to children in the North." They were reprimanded or accorded approval "in the name of ancestors and continuing family traditions . . . supported by unique patterns of cousin intermarriage and preservation of family lore."

Individual family households often include members beyond parents and children. It was typical until around 1940 for the survivor to remain in the family home after the death of the spouse and to be joined by a child with spouse and children in tow. Sometimes, a great-grandparent also lived in the house.

Although it is no longer practiced, a sometimes-practiced pre–World War I custom in the Upper Cumberland required that fathers "set free" their sons when they reached the age of twenty-one. Ward Curtis, born in Monroe County in 1900, recalled vividly when his own father released him two years early: "My father set me free when I was nineteen. Most daddies waited 'til their sons was twenty-one, but Daddy told me, 'I'm setting you free now. Two more years would take up too much of your time.' He set us boys free at nineteen. That means that you were a man of your own head; he wasn't your boss no more. But now I didn't set my own boys free. Times had changed by then."

The practice of choosing a marriage partner from one's own community or a nearby one was almost always followed before World War I. Marriage to a neighbor or distant relative was often a matter of sheer convenience. Too, such an arrangement was universally sanctioned because it provided for social and economic stability, ensuring a continuing recognition of kinship and devotion to one's own people and to the larger community.

Living adjacent to parents or grandparents on the same parcel of land was also typical, even for tenant families. Young marrieds were encouraged to settle down and build homes close to their parents. The term "weaning house" was sometimes applied to these nearby dwellings, especially in Russell and Wayne counties, Kentucky.

Once the newlyweds had settled into their home, each of them was

A Cumberland
Plateau man and his
grandchildren, 1946
(Photo courtesy of
Tennessee State Library
and Archives)

expected to act in accordance with the roles that their families and others in the community had come to expect. The woman's work comprised cooking, housekeeping chores, vegetable gardening and, during pre-1900 years, carding wool and cotton and tanning the leather used in making items of clothing worn by family members. Other female tasks included quilting, doing the family laundry on a scrub board, and, along with the children, milking the cows and gathering the eggs. At hog-killing time, the woman was responsible for canning and preserving much of the meat, rendering the lard, and making lye soap. At night, when the supper dishes had been washed and put away, she busied herself mending clothes, peeling apples, stringing beans, or working at some other task in preparation for the next day.

Except for teaching school, women rarely sought employment outside the home before the 1940s. Those who did venture into the public sector filled positions such as postmaster, school superintendent, bank clerk, and nurse. However, women who worked outside the home were still expected to do the bulk of domestic chores and care for the children. It would be hard to make a claim that men in the region worked longer and harder each day than women.

Wives frequently went into the fields to help their husbands with crop cultivation, especially when older daughters were around to do the housework and to care for young children. It was not uncommon for parents to take their babies and small children to the field, put them on a quilt brought along for the purpose, and place a trusted canine referred to as a "snakedog" with the little ones to guard them. Even when pregnant, most women continued their farm and home chores right up until the time their babies were born. Women seldom complained about having to do fieldwork, but apparently very few men returned the favor by helping their wives with domestic chores.

Men busied themselves farming, trapping fur-bearing animals, and hunting rabbits, squirrels, possum, groundhogs, and migratory fowl, as well as maintaining shelter for animals and caring for sick creatures. During winter months, they spent much time whittling out and smoothing ax handles, hammer handles, wooden spoons, and trays.

Children helped with the planting of seeds, weeding the garden, feeding chickens, splitting and carrying in stovewood, taking out the wood ashes, feeding hogs, suckering tobacco, making soap, washing dishes, and sharpening kitchen knives, among a host of other easy-to-do but detested jobs. It was common practice for young girls no older than seven or eight to be assigned cooking duties and household chores once an older sister got married. Along with their parents, children got up at four in the morning, summer and winter.

The job of child-rearing fell to both parents, though the father's role was less clearly defined than the mother's. Whereas in urban settings the father was gone from the home for most of the day to do industrial work, families in the Upper Cumberland, being largely rural, tended to work together at major tasks. The father served as both ceremonial figurehead and presumably as the ultimate arbiter in family matters, especially those of an economic nature. However, day-to-day care and discipline of the children fell to the mother. Margaret Hagood, writing about southern tenant mothers, makes observations that are certainly appropriate to motherhood in the Upper Cumberland. Hagood comments that "mothers enjoy telling about raising children and most of them seem well satisfied with the results. . . . Most of the women recognize child-raising as a mother's most serious responsibility and yet they still treat it humorously, as did one mother who said, 'How do I raise my children? I pulls them right up by the hair of their head!' "

Even when married, young women were left uneducated in matters pertaining to sex, pregnancy, and childbearing. Before there were hospitals, and in those areas not readily accessible to physicians, women in childbirth were often assisted by their husbands or perhaps another, usually much older, woman in the community. Known today as mid-wives, these trusted, well-respected women were usually called "aunts."

One of these women who was somewhat atypical was Aunt Matt Brooks, a black woman from Gainesboro, well-known as a midwife at the time and still legendary. Matt worked for Dr. Fowler, a white physician, during the late years of the nineteenth century. According to local tradition, Dr. Fowler's son, Charlie, always escorted Matt to town. On

An Upper Cumberland child learning at an early age how to help with home, farm, and garden chores, ca. 1972 (Photo by David Sutherland)

the way, he always gave her "two or three shots of whiskey to get her to feel good," said Landon Anderson, a native of Gainesboro. "And she had this dapper blue horse that could rack. Boy, he could rack!

"When they got out there by Bybee's Mill," Anderson went on, "Charlie would give her the last drink, and he'd say, 'Get up, Matt.' She'd stand up in that saddle and she'd come through town a-hollering and that horse just a-flying!"

Early physicians in the Upper Cumberland demonstrated considerable respect for midwives, fully expecting them to take charge of the birthing process when isolation and distance precluded the presence of a licensed medical doctor. Dr. W. F. Owsley of Burkesville who, at age ninety-eight was the oldest still-practicing physician in the region in 1975, described with respect the work of midwives. He also commented on the physical stamina and determination of numerous pregnant women during the early years of the twentieth century, describing one woman who gave birth to twins while standing at the spring in front of a washtub and another who returned to the tobacco field less than two weeks after her child was born. In a humorous vein, Dr. Owsley told about the time he spent the remainder of the night at the home of a woman he had just delivered. At daybreak the next morning, he was sitting around sipping a cup of coffee when someone said, "Doc, breakfast is ready."

"And I went and set down at the table," Owsley said. "Then I heard this voice say, 'Have a biscuit.' And it was the woman I had just delivered."

There was a wide range of folk beliefs and practices surrounding pregnancy and childbirth. A mother could prevent second and subsequent pregnancies by extending periods of breast feeding. That babies could be "marked" was an extremely common belief. Marking might be the result of the mother's cravings for food or drink or of something that gave her a great fright. It was thought that if an expectant mother saw an animal die or a human corpse, her child would have unsightly birthmarks.

A common belief was that, with the onset of the birthing process, labor pain (and afterpain as well) could be cut by the placing of a sharp-bladed instrument under the woman's bed. When the infant was born, the afterbirth should be sprinkled with salt and then either burned or buried. Extreme care should be taken to prevent a dog from getting hold of the placenta, lest the mother have a resultant lifelong physical disability. A baby born with a veil (caul) over its face would see ghosts and other spirit-world entities later in life.

Numerous other beliefs and practices were called into play during the process of rearing a child. For example, cutting a baby's fingernails or hair before it was a year old would result in the child's ongoing bad luck. Nails should be bitten off by a parent. A baby that did not fall off the bed before it reached its first birthday would die during childhood, and a similar fate awaited a little one who talked before it walked. Some beliefs are still part of local life and culture, such as the notion that a cat left alone with a baby will suck the baby's breath and kill it, or that tickling a child's feet will cause it to stutter.

During the weaning process, it was common for a mother to chew food for her baby and then place it in the child's mouth. Too, she frequently prepared a sugar teat by wrapping sugar, or a sugar and butter mixture, in a piece of white cloth in the shape of a nipple. Catnip tea induced sleep in babies and was also good for them during periods of sickness. A child's playing with fire at nighttime was sure to induce bedwetting. Such a habit could be broken if the child's face was rubbed with its own wet bedclothes. And since virtually all children were born at home before World War II, parents told an inquisitive child that they found it in a hollow log, under a big cabbage leaf, in a briar patch, or, according to Hugh Yates of Columbia, "the buzzard laid an egg on a big flat rock and the sun hatched you." Storks were seldom mentioned and hospitals were unheard of except as places where people went to die.

During early childhood years, Upper Cumberland children often clung to their baby dolls and other toddler playthings. At the same time, these youngsters began using numerous homemade objects for play purposes. Such toys were made by the youngsters themselves or their parents or grandparents from nature's materials or from scrap items found around the house. Homecrafted items were especially important during early times when money was scarce or unavailable.

As these pre-1940 youngsters grew into older childhood, they were often compelled to rely on their own skill and ingenuity, as parents' energies were devoted to babies and small children or to the adult world of work. Toys made by older children, along with traditional gestures and mimicry, were accurate mirrors of the adult world. Their items of play were replicas of real objects used by adults in daily life routines. These handmade toys served the same function for children as tools did for adults.

Folklorist Simon J. Bronner makes a strong claim that these folklore items, both material and verbal, reflect a division between adulthood, where authority resides, and childhood, where the youngsters are still under parental control. Children, Bronner asserts, have a powerful urge and need to declare their own identity. Thus it is that their shared folklore is a peer-protected expression of cultural connection to one another. As these young ones continue the maturing process, they "fiercely hang on to their cultural property to express their distinct personality and social separation from other ages," both younger and older. Children increasingly left to themselves used folklore as part of the maturing process.

Whether intentionally or unconsciously, older children mimicked their parents and other adults in the community by pretending to smoke cigarettes, pipes, and cigars fashioned from sticks and corncobs, by carving out make-believe guns for use in stalking imaginary wild animals, and by wearing their mother's dresses and shoes or their father's hats or other clothing. The variety and quality of these children's playthings were limited only by the imagination and crafting skills of their creators.

Such objects of play were employed by the young members of the family in slack working times and on churchless Sundays, which, for most rural youth, meant three free Sundays each month. Because of the distances between homes, children and their families sometimes had to rely on their own ingenuity, creativity, and the potential for fun afforded by their immediate environment. Older children living within a three-mile radius of each other, however, managed to get together rather frequently for periods of play and recreation not associated with school activities.

The toys they used fell into two broad categories. One included those items that satisfied individual recreational needs, such as paper cut-outs (usually from a mail-order catalog); cornstalk or hickory-limb flutter mills placed in a stream of water to imitate real water mills; buzzers (made by the placing of buttons on a string); whistles made from river or creekbottom reeds (a child would place blades of grass between the thumbs and blow on the grass or simply cup the hands together and blow between the thumbs); soap-bubble blowers (generally corncob pipes); and redbud leaves, which could be popped if a child cupped them one at a time into a cavity made by one hand and hit them with a resounding blow with the open palm of the other.

The second category comprises all forms of play involving skill, dexterity, and rough-and-tumble competition. Toys and playthings in this group were of two basic varieties—those that were not life-threatening if misused and those that were.

The non-threatening toys and games, in addition to those mentioned in the first category, included mumblety peg and marbles, kicking the can, riding stick horses, walking on stilts, pushing a metal wheel by means of a u-shaped hoop fashioned from a Prince Albert or Velvet tobacco can, riding or pulling a heavy-duty "truck wagon" that was fashioned from materials as hand (the four wheels were made from sawed-off sections of black-gum or oak logs), and playing with balls made either from rubber inner tubes wrapped with cotton string or from the bladders of butchered hogs. The latter functioned as volley balls when inflated by air blown through a quill made from a "pipe stem" (joint of wild cane) inserted into the opening in the bladder, which was then allowed to dry. Some children of the Upper Cumberland saved these bladder balls until Christmas morning when they were burst open with a loud popping noise.

Among the truly dangerous toys was the slingshot. In early times, the slingshot had the traditional leather cradle fastened at the ends of two strings. The cradle held rocks that could be thrown at a target, usually an animal. In later years, especially after the introduction of rubber inner tubes for automobile tires, it was common practice to affix two strips of rubber either to a small, handcarved wooden frame with a handhold beneath the opening, or to a forked branch from a dogwood tree that also had a handhold beneath. A leather cradle that nested the object to be projected was attached at the extended ends of the two rubber strips. A small round rock or a lead ball such as a ball bearing were typical projectiles shot at targets such as birds, rabbits, and squirrels.

"Shooting" the slingshot involves holding it firmly by the handle with one hand while the other grasps the cradled projectile and stretches the rubber strips until they are taut and aimed at the target. At the opportune moment, the hunter releases the rubbers and projectile, which speeds toward the target with such force that a human being standing in the path could easily be knocked unconscious or perhaps killed.

Other dangerous play activities included shooting homecrafted bows and arrows (arrows were made from sharpened wooden stakes or horseshoe nails, the heads of which had been pounded and flattened, then wrapped around the wooden stakes); hurling wet corncobs at others with intent to injure; shooting "pop guns" loaded with wet paper wads or large seeds from wild trees and bushes at others in face-to-face combat; swinging out over bluffs and swimming holes on a grapevine; and riding down steep, snow-covered slopes on sleds with runners greased with lye soap to enhance speed.

Dangerous or not, such childhood toys and playthings were social tools in the truest sense of the word. They were instrumental in the establishment and continuity of sibling relationships from early years until marriage, or when employment in a distant southern or midwestern city brought about disruption in the family social order. Too, these instruments of play served as bonding agents for community youngsters who used them as excuses on holidays and weekends for walking several miles to visit and socialize with friends in their houses, yards, or barns. There was a toy or play object that served every social need.

Though these gatherings with childhood friends were valued, fellowship and fun within the family unit were important, especially during winter months when romping across hillsides, hunting birds and rabbits, and swinging out across swimming holes were all precluded by cold, ice, and snow. At such times family members engaged in games of checkers, swapout (seeing which player could get rid of his or her checkers first), and cards.

Summer months found family members at work on the back porch preparing garden vegetables and orchard fruits for canning and on the front porch visiting with neighbors and passers-by. Such periods of socializing fostered a sense of belonging through general conversation about neighbors, the recounting of stories about ancestors and the supernatural, and the telling of humorous anecdotes.

The sense of tightly knit family, both immediate and extended, also embraces the past, incorporating all those persons who ever felt an affinity with the family. Narratives told within the family circle accord satisfaction to their tellers and listeners alike by providing historical information about family roots while creating generational identity for today's members. While some family narratives told in the region may be contemporary, most stories are passed along from one generation to the next. In the Upper Cumberland, where identity with the land is very strong, family folklore is a relection of strong ties to the land itself and to the past generations who, in numerous instances, owned and occupied the same place. It is still possible to find families here, six and seven

Dora K. Murray and Dorothy Farris of Burkesville share recollections of growing up black in the Upper Cumberland. (Photo by Greg Lyuch)

generations removed from the original settlers, living on the land staked out by these progenitors.

It is usually not necessary to drill children with the names of their ancestors, since family stories, especially those that reach back through one's great-grandparents, are studded with real names. Such accounts may provide a humorous twist to family history, telling how a particular person came to be named or to be portrayed as a heroic figure. Certain families in the Persimon-Stringtown-Rock Bridge area of northern Monroe County know well the legend of their Union soldier ancestor "Old Billy Clemons," who reputedly shot and killed his commanding officer and was hanged by his thumbs for a period of time as punishment. Clemons's neighbor, William "Pick" Strode, was so named because "he could pick up more brush from a freshly cleared newground than anyone else." Pick Strode's daughter, Canzadie, who died of consumption (tuberculosis) at age seventeen, is remembered in kinship circles because of her deathbed request to be buried on the hill overlooking the family's house because she didn't "want to be too far from home."

The descendants of Eliza Jane Harris Witty tell how she single-handedly drove a team of horses hooked to a covered wagon from Kentucky to Kansas in the 1890s. Passengers included her tuberculosis-ridden husband Bird Witty, who had heard that the Kansas plains offered a surefire cure for his ailment, and their three small children. Not long after arrival there, Eliza took Bird to a doctor, only to be advised to begin the return trip to Kentucky soon if her husband desired to be buried in his homeland. She brought him back to southern Kentucky shortly thereafter, and he died six weeks later at age thirty-eight.

Such narratives, typically non-chronologically oriented, are referred to as family sagas by Texan Mody Boatwright, who defines them as a form of lore that accumulates around families, often the patriarch or matriarch, and is preserved and modified by oral transmission. The events described in such sagas, Boatwright says, reflect the family's social values and thus may not always describe accurately what really happened. Nonetheless, the stories are accepted at face value, functioning in the life of the family as strong bonding agents for past and present generations and creating meaningful identity for individual family members.

Social events surrounding special days such as birthdays, Easter, Memorial Day, and Christmas typically involve all members of the family unit, including grandparents. Birthdays are celebrated in whatever manner is most meaningful to the individual. Although nowadays the celebrant is showered with presents, in earlier years gifts were rather rare. The event was marked in other ways, however. A once-common ritual act involved forcibly putting the birthday person under the dining table. In another rite of passage, the celebrant was spanked one time for every year of age, plus "one [spank] to grow on." The birthday cake, sometimes with candles, sometimes without, was and still is an ever-present part of the festivities.

Easter was both a family and a community affair in that three or four families often shared in the annual hunt for multi-colored eggs that had been hidden by one or more adults. Easter egg hunts were held by some church groups as well, according to Cander Williams, a black resident of Cumberland County, Kentucky. Preparations for the big event began two or three days before Easter, when the women and older girls boiled and colored the eggs to be used. The eggs were either dipped into bowls of colored water or given circular designs with crayolas or pencils with colored leads. Often one goose egg was colored and hidden with the hen eggs; its finder won a special prize.

Children ran hither and yon looking for the eggs, screaming with delight each time they found a hidden treasure. Family dogs often shared in the festivities, taking part both in the search and in consuming the bounty after the hunt, when their young masters sat around peeling and eating the eggs they had found.

Decoration Day has been especially significant in the Upper Cumberland since its inception following the Civil War. Even now when the custom of memorializing the dead is in decline, this special day serves as a reminder of specific people and events identified with the families and communities across the region. Tales and tellers of tales await those who make the annual pilgrimages to the graves of persons who, if not remembered personally, are known from the stories still recounted about them.

The placing of floral tributes on the graves is still a form of ritual behavior. Each grave is adorned by family members who are often no closer kin than cousins once or twice removed. Virtually every gravesite receives an offering of flowers, which may vary from year to year according to the donors' color preferences. Siblings often jointly donate money toward the purchase of flowers for a deceased mother or father so as to ensure that their tribute will be as nice as anybody else's.

Most community-based cemeteries now have endowments, or "perpetual funds," as they are called locally. Contributions to these accounts help to guarantee that a paid custodial crew will clean and maintain the cemetery a specified number of times each season. Family burial plots do not typically have endowments, however, and thus rely for cleaning once or twice each year on combined family efforts.

Memorial Day services are held annually in numerous cemeteries across the Upper Cumberland. Leaders from the local community or persons who now live elsewhere and have returned for the commemorative services are called on to lead the ceremonial proceedings. One or more persons will "make a few comments" about the importance of Memorial Day (also locally called Decoration Day, or simply "the Thirtieth") and of cemetery maintenance before asking everyone present to contribute as liberally as possible.

Like Memorial Day, Christmas has always been a major holiday at school and at home in the region. Letters to Santa have been a part of the Christmas celebration for as long as living generations can remember, though they were not "mailed" to the North Pole until recent times. In my own childhood, letters to Santa were held at the rear of the fireplace opening with one hand, generally a parent's or grandparent's, and fanned until they were sucked into the warm current of air and carried upward through the chimney en route to Santa and his helpers.

Christmas trees were largely unheard of until the 1920s. Stockings were generally hung by the fireplace. And while a few toys found their

Many community cemeteries in the Upper Cumberland still have no endowed custodial funds. (Photo by the author)

way into stockings at that time, children soon learned not to expect too much in this regard. Nonetheless, it was still a big thrill for children to jump out of bed on Christmas morning, dash across the cold floor, grab their stockings from the mantlepiece and head back to their warm beds, rubbing the mysterious bumps in the stockings and wondering what they were.

Many natives of the Upper Cumberland born before 1940 did not exchange gifts at Christmas. That came later. Only children received gifts. People of earlier generations also remember having out-of-season fruit only at Christmas each year. An entire stalk of bananas was often found hanging from the ceiling on Christmas Eve night or Christmas morning. Children and adults alike ate them slowly so as to savor the wonderful taste as long as possible. A bushel basket of red or yellow apples, and perhaps a bag of oranges as well, might be found in the homes of those residents who could afford the luxury of fruit.

Singing was a regular part of everyday life for many families in the Upper Cumberland, especially when a fiddle, banjo, or guitar could be played by one or more family members. Other families did a lot of singing without the instruments during the workday and around the fireplace in the evenings. This trend became even more pronounced when the extremely popular shape-note gospel songbooks became available shortly after 1900. Numerous oral testimonies tell of four-part harmony family ensembles that sang around the hearth during winter months and under the shadetree in the yard during summer months, often with neighbors joining in.

Pump organs or pianos were found in many Upper Cumberland homes, especially those of land-owning families, and by the late 1920s phonographs were owned by some of the well-to-do families, who often invited neighbors and friends from the community in to listen to the music provided by the cylinder recordings.

Aside from the automobile, introduced at about the same time, the battery-powered radio had the greatest social impact on the Upper Cumberland. Typically, it was the World War I veterans who, by virtue of their small monthly pension checks, were able to afford these "wonder boxes." Neighbors from the entire community gathered on Saturday nights at one of the two or three radio-equipped homes to listen to the broadcasts. Carlos Pitcock, resident of the Cumberland River community known as the Elbow, located in eastern Monroe County, recalled that "everyone up and down Pitcock Branch would come to our house every Saturday night to hear the Grand Ole Opry from eight o'clock 'til twelve midnight. And the house would just be plumb full from one end to the other. Didn't have enough chairs, you know, and just sat around on the floor."

Youngsters and adults alike were present at such gatherings during the 1930s. Usually not present, however, were male and female teenagers and young adults. Like their peers in generations past, these young people often gathered someplace else, engaging in traditional forms of play and courtship. These were the same youngsters who had played and conspired together during their early years and had retained close ties as they grew toward maturity. But now their socializing was done in the form of courtship games such as candy breakings, pea and bean shellings, and corn huskings. Such activities were especially popular socially and as courtship practices before 1920.

Candy breakings were social gatherings sometimes held for mercenary reasons by the host. Sticks of candy were identified individually, each bearing the name of one of the girls present. The candy was then auctioned off, as was done at pie and box suppers, with the fellow making the highest bid getting both the candy stick and the girl. Most of the time, however, candy breakings were scheduled so that the area's young people could just come together and have a good time. Sometimes the candy stick was broken in two so that both boy and girl could each have half a stick. Other times the couple would sit face to face eating away at the unbroken stick of candy. Naturally, their lips would touch as they partook of the last bite.

Candy breakings were always followed by music and games. Games played by young adults during the pre–1920 era included dumb supper (a game in which a young woman prepared a meal in silence and awaited the arrival of a male to sit in a chair by her), spin the top (a form of social activity in which an object would be returned to its rightful owner only after the owner had performed commands such as "crow like a rooster" or "sing a song about . . ."), scat (a game in which all the fellows left the room and the girls told which one they would like to occupy the vacant chair beside them; if the returning boy chose correctly, the girl said, "Stuck"; if he was wrong, she yelled out, "Scat!"), and cherry tree, a singing game in which two fellows linked arms and marched around a ring singing, "The higher you climb a cherry tree, the riper are the berries; the more the young man courts that girl, the sooner they shall marry." Each boy then chose a girl from the circle.

The most popular activity for those of courtship age, however, was the play-party, a form of handholding, waistgrabbing activity acceptable even to the most religiously austere people of the community, who banned all forms of dance as tools of Satan. These lively events, held in area homes during winter months, were performed without the use of musical instruments. Words to these dance-like games were sung by the participants who often clapped their hands as a means of pacing body movements. Such events typically lasted from about midnight to two in the morning. L. L. McDowell provides one of the clearest statements as to the mechanics of these play-parties:

These old games [such as Candy Gal and Skip to my Lou] were essentially group dances, and the principal idea was the pattern of the group movement; a set of figures through which the whole group moved in time to the words and music of the song; all the changes being timed by the words. There was no instrumental music. . . . Often, there was a game or contest embodied in the dance, the object usually being the securing of a partner.

Daily Crouch of Moodyville, Pickett County, noted that these gala events were held primarily in wintertime. "We lived in these old log houses, and our parents would let us take all the furniture down in one room," Crouch said. "And we'd get out here in the community and gather in boys and girls and have a big play."

Dancing parties were very popular as early as the mid-nineteenth century. A. L. Dale of Celina writes of these events in his unpublished memoirs:

It was fashionable then [mid-1850s] to have dancing parties at the homes. . . . We would dance all night very often and when the dance would break up, the young ladies were accompanied home by their parents. It would fall my lot to be caller at the dancing and to decide upon the next place to have a dance.

By the early years of the twentieth century, community dances were even less formal. Numerous people recalled attending square dances that lasted throughout the night. The Lillydale area of Clay County was renowned for such dance events. "We did a lot of square dancing around Lillydale," wrote a former resident. "Almost every Saturday night during the winter months someone moved the furniture out of one or two large rooms and all night long the rafters rang with 'The Virginia Reel,' 'Blue Beads,' 'Shoot the Buffalo,' and many others."

It was not uncommon for husband-wife teams to play instruments on these occasions, with the woman typically serving as banjoist.

Fiddle and banjo players, both black and white, were plentiful across the Upper Cumberland, fiddlers more so. And because of population inequity, white musicians were more common than blacks. Some of the known old-time black musicians who played at family and community functions included banjo pickers Cal and John Coe of the Zeketown community, located in southern Cumberland County, Kentucky, the same county that is remembered for the black Huddleston family musicians in the Marrowbone vicinity. Black musicians from Clinton County included Claud and Osby Jones, guitarist and banjoist, respectively, from the Crocus community. Clinton County's New Hope community produced the black Burchett brothers, who typically played in private homes without pay but, because of their strong Christian convictions, "didn't tolerate dancing and the like," according to their nephew, Sanford Sprowls. However, they did take part in the music and song contests held through the 1930s either in the Cumberland County courthouse yard or inside if there was rain. White musicians were not included in the day's events, although they, along with a host of other whites, were always present in the audience, according to Sprowls. "Strictly blacks against blacks," he said. "Awfulest crowds present there ever was."

Across the state line in Tennessee, an old-time black string band comprising members of the Sadler family originated in the Granville area of Jackson County in the 1920s. The Sadlers continued to play for area dances well into the 1950s.

The racially integrated Tick community of Jackson County produced the black Farris brothers in the early years of this century. Also from Jackson County was Martin Gore, a highly polished fiddle player from Gainesboro.

Other old-time black musicians of the early square-dance era included three Bertram brothers, along with Marion Redmon, from the Wolf River Valley of Pickett County.

Black or white, these old-time musicians were highly respected artists wherever they were heard. They played at barber shops, pie suppers, square dances, homecomings, and other informal gatherings. Often, some of these performers were invited into private homes for an evening of music and song when square dancing was not part of the scene; for example, white musician Joe Jackson of Burnside and his daughter Madeline preferred to entertain with their banjo and guitar without attendant dancing.

Sometimes fiddle or banjo music was played for children who were present. Hiram Parrish, a white resident of Burkesville, shared this memory from his childhood:

I recall this old man John Richard Scott, who lived down in the river bottom. Had a great, long beard. Us boys would go down there to visit, because he had a boy about our age. We'd go down there and play in the branch, make little boats and rafts and flutter mills; just play in the branch.

Then, when we'd get tired we'd go to the house where it was warm. Mrs. Scott said, "Now, Mr. Scott, I think you ought to play the boys a few tunes."

And, boy, could he make it talk!

The Johnson Family Band of Gainesboro, headed up by Henry "Pap" Johnson, was one of the most popular old-time dance and concert bands in the region. From the early 1920s until the early 1940s, the Johnson Family Band played at schools, picnics, and other social functions, winning a large following of fans in the process. The band was known for its interpretations of such numbers as "Coming 'Round the Mountain," "Father, Dear Father, Come Home With Me Now," "Wildwood Flower," "Bile Them Cabbage Down," "Noah's Ark," "Chinese Breakdown," "Over the Waves," and "San Antonio Rose."

John G. Campbell of Albany provided a list of old-time dance bands active in that part of the region from 1912 to the early 1950s, at which time "canned music" began to dominate the local dance scene. These early ensembles were identified by their musicians rather than by a specific name, with Campbell himself a chief participant. Others included such renowned musicians as Blind Dick Burnett of Wayne County, the oldest professional musician in the Upper Cumberland until his death in 1977.

It is apparent from talking with numerous persons about the early square dances that heavy drinking and brawling were not a part of such social gatherings, especially those before and just after the turn of the twentieth century. Edith Williams of Celina noted that "if Christians went to square dances they were criticized, but they was still a lot of dancing back then. It wasn't like it is now. They were well chaperoned; not many fights or drinking."

Carlos Storie of Pickett County supported her position. "They'd have dinner and dance and sing songs back then," he remembered. "They just enjoyed that back then. Nobody didn't get drunk and cause no trouble. But nowadays they can't have one. There's always somebody that'd have to tear it up."

Old-time fiddler Keen Bradley of Willow Grove in Clay County was known, respected, and hosted by numerous families on both sides of the state line. Bradley was an educated fellow who played classical violin and taught school for several years before becoming a wandering minstrel. People of the Cumberland River counties remember him not only for his expertise on the fiddle but for his guitar, piano, and French harp playing as well. He survived through the generosity of the friends and neighbors for whom he played. Bradley "was such a good musician that people would invite him into their homes," Mae Goff of Cumberland County claimed. "Their children enjoyed it and they treated him with respect. He'd just come up on his horse and sometimes stay for a week at a time." Although he never volunteered manual labor, Bradley helped children with their school lessons and made music for people as long as they were willing to listen. People who put Bradley up in their homes always supplied him and his horse with food and shelter.

Various other old-time musicians roamed the countryside in search of food and shelter, always with a fiddle or banjo tucked under their arms or across their backs by means of a belt. "None of these old-time musicians had a home fit to live in; just lived in a hollow tree," claimed Frazier Moss of Jackson County, who learned his own musical skills from itinerant banjo and fiddle players.

Moss himself first began to play the fiddle in 1918 at the age of eight. His first fiddle came from Ferry's Seed Company as a prize for the large amount of garden seeds he had sold. To his chagrin, the fiddle was a toy. Nonetheless, young Moss strung it with his mother's sewing thread, tuned it, and learned to play it. In later years, especially in the 1960s and 1970s, Moss won numerous national fiddle championships.

Whether or not musicians were present, picnics were extremely popular with young people of courtship age in the days before the automobile. Virtually every community had a favorite spot where picnics were held, but some particularly stand out in the participants' memories. Bee Rock, south of Monterey, and Bald Rock, located in extreme southeastern Clinton County adjacent to the Tennessee state line, were popular spots. Young people for miles around gathered at these special places on Sundays to pick wildflowers and spread their basket lunches out on the large, bare rock outcroppings.

After play-parties, dances, or picnics were over, the participants walked home, rode horseback, or traveled in buggies, much as they did following attendance at revival or church services. Roy Deckard of Monroe County described what took place on the way home after a religious event had ended for the evening:

After the services, the fellows would hurry up and gang up outside and wait for the girls to come out. Then they'd walk up to the girl they wanted to walk home and say, "The moon shines bright, may I see you home tonight?"

And if she wanted to go with that particular fellow, she'd say, "Well, the stars shine, too; I don't mind if I do."

That meant they had a date. He'd walk her home. Didn't have no car. She'd walk on one side of the road and him on the other.

Lots of times you'd stand at the gate and talk, or at the front door. Sometimes, if her parents were willing, you could go inside awhile.

The young men of each community often ran in groups, primarily to protect their territorial rights when fellows from other communities tried to make inroads. They frequently carried guns, mainly for bluffing, but "would use them if necessary," according to Ward Curtis of eastern Monroe County. One of their favorite activities was to hide alongside the road and throw rocks at any outsider who dared try to court a local girl.

A chaperone often accompanied each couple, as parents expected their daughters to be shielded against potential surrender to human frailty. Paternal shielding of daughters was especially common in many communities of the Upper Cumberland. During a taped interview, Sherman Burnett of Sunnybrook, Wayne County, stated five times in as many minutes that "fathers watched out for their daughters." Many others agreed with Burnett. Gladys Norton Meadows of Free State, Jackson County, said that in her courtship years during the early 1920s "young people socialized by visiting in their front yards or going to dances in some of their homes." Meadows then told how her father arranged for her marriage to take place inside the Norton family home so that she would not leave the house in the company of her husband-to-be until they were actually married. Her father's actions were prompted by the elopement of her older sister.

On matters pertaining to pre-marital sex, some mothers, knowing the importance of restraint and chastity, sometimes voiced their concern over a son's behavior. Nonetheless, such words of admonition did not prevent a young man from going out, often to seek pleasure from a girl in the community. Even though contraceptive practices were largely unknown or rejected among the younger set, however, pregnancies out of wedlock were not very common. Lynnie White of Monticello wrote that girls who became pregnant before marriage were said to have been "ruined or fooled." White commented on the community's double standard regarding these instances. "Those good pioneer women . . . forgave the man; it was no more than they expected of a man. It was a girl's job to keep a man in his place, and they didn't forgive her if she didn't. . . . A man could run off to Texas or somewhere until it died down; all that was left for the girl to do was to stay at home and wait on the rest of the family or marry some old man needing a wife to wait on him."

Pre–World War I courtships often began when the girl was rather young and did not last very long, as marriage soon ensued. The man was typically a few years older than the woman. Once they decided to get married, elopement was frequently looked upon as the easiest, most practical way to wed, especially when the bride-to-be was under age. Church weddings were rare, especially in rural areas, though couples who chose not to elope were often married by a minister in his home or at some other agreed-upon place.

Since honeymoons were only for the rich folk, the newlyweds' first night together was generally spent at the place where they would be starting their new life. Whether or not this was a private abode mattered little to other residents of the community. Noisy merrymaking—a shivaree—was a must!

Attendance at such events often included as many as fifty persons, each bent on making more noise than the others by yelling, shouting, and using such instruments as cowbells, sheep bells, school bells, dinner bells, tin pans and buckets, fox horns, guns fired ceaselessly at a safe distance from the house, and hammers beaten on a circular saw taken from a local sawmill and carried by two fellows holding onto the ends of an iron rod supporting the saw. The evening of revelry usually broke up with the groom being taken for a ride on a fence rail and the blushing bride carted around in a wash tub. These free rides were sure to come if the couple had failed to make adequate provision for passing out drinks and treats of food to the funmakers.

When members of the courtship age married and had children of their own, a new life cycle began. But life went on for the parent generation, as they entered new and different social activities throughout their lives. Finally, when death came the parents would be replaced by their children and their children's children.

It would not be fair to view family structure in the Upper Cumberland as overwhelmingly patriarchal in those early years. Women as well as men were key players in perpetuating the prevailing social structures, and their empowerment did not wait until the recent feminist movement. The distinction between gender roles, economic power, and spiritual leadership in the Upper Cumberland, yet to be described by scholars, would be more clearly understood through in-depth analyses of the day-by-day activities of the region's families, then and now.

Family and community kinship ties, religion, agrarianism, and traditional ways of thinking and acting continued to influence life in the Upper Cumberland for much of the first half of the twentieth century. These same social agents still affect regional consciousness and the practical aspects of family life, contributing to a strong sense of place for everyone who has ever called the Upper Cumberland home. The family remains a fundamental source of regional identity and, by and large, continues to be a chief means by which the concept of community can be articulated.

However, the presence of stereo and compact disc recorders and television, along with a host of kitchen amenities, has altered some families' routines, such as how the evening hours are spent. This part of the day may not be as memorable as it was before technology and its attendant entertainment and labor-saving devices were available. The regimen of sun-up to sun-down work in the fields and never-ending household chores was a wearing daily schedule. Present times may consist of equally difficult routines. Unlike those earlier families that relished the social time between supper and bed, contemporary families may not be as eager for such interaction, preferring instead to spend time with stereos, videocamcorders, boats, and stock cars.

Schools and Churches as Community Social Agents

Following the family unit in importance were the local schools and churches, which played a crucial part in the democratization process, especially with the proliferation of public schools during the twenty-year period following the Civil War. Until that time, less well-to-do families had not been able to afford the modest tuition costs required to send their children to the small, semi-private subscription schools. While churches were based on the precept that all persons were created as equals, some families in the region did not attend church at all, either because they did not feel welcome or did not have adequate clothing to wear in public; nevertheless, both institutions deeply affected the lives of most Upper Cumberland residents.

COMMUNITY SCHOOLS

The first efforts to establish uniform school systems in the Upper Cumberland area were initiated when state legislative bodies sought to unify educational processes in their respective domains. In 1806 Tennessee enacted a law providing for the establishment of academies and the appointment of trustees to governing boards for each of the new institutions. Kentucky followed suit. By 1808 the legislature had passed acts calling for the establishment of private academies on public lands of the commonwealth. Many academies were thus established in the Upper Cumberland at an early date on both sides of the state line. These institutions, often called subscription schools, were supported largely by parents who paid tuition of from one to four dollars for each child who attended them primarily to help absorb the costs of hiring teachers and maintaining the buildings.

The 1830s witnessed the dawning of state-supported educational systems in both Tennessee and Kentucky. Both state legislatures appropriated funds for education in the early 1820s; however, it was not until about 1830 in Tennessee and 1836 in Kentucky that the public education system even gained a tenuous position. Education in Kentucky and Tennessee continued along much the same lines from the 1830s until around 1870 and from that time until around 1910.

Throughout the nineteenth century, free schools were taught only during the fall months. Their subscription school counterparts were usually held in the spring. Teachers, especially those in the free schools, were typically people who had been born in the community. Local overseers were responsible for the hiring of teachers, the maintenance of the school buildings, and the rules governing student conduct. Free public education extended only through the eighth grade, with secondary education provided by private academies. And while a few state-supported high schools were founded in the Upper Cumberland shortly after the turn of the century, most of them were established just before and after World War I.

Attendance was not mandatory, so enrollment was generally minimal. The first freshman class of Pickett County, in 1922, comprised six students—three girls and three boys. Only the girls were present at graduation four years later; the fellows had all dropped out along the way.

Education for blacks was practically nil until after the Civil War. Within three years laws were passed levying a school tax for Negro education, but the tax was so meager that only the poorest facilities could be afforded. A former Wayne County school superintendent, Ira Bell, described the numerous black elementary schools in his county as having been "constructed out of poles and shacks . . . , truly pitiful things to look at." The few blacks across the region who graduated from the eighth grade and wished to attend high school were sent away at state expense to boarding schools elsewhere, generally out of the region. Exceptions to the rule were black high schools located in Carthage and Monticello. To the credit of white people in the region, when the United States Supreme Court ruled in 1954 that racial segregation must cease, schools in the Upper Cumberland integrated without major incident. Seniors in both Jackson and Russell counties elected black students as presidents of their classes that year.

Much has been made of the democracy that was cultivated by the one-room community school, whether attended by blacks or whites. In general, these small institutions served farm areas, where there were two loosely developed castes: the land-owners and the tenant farmers. Caste lines were rarely perceptible in the little community school. It was seldom asked what sort of homes children had come from if they could run faster than the other children in the school, or spell down their class,

A former one-room school building at Hacker's Branch, northwestern Monroe County (Photo by the author)

or solve the most complicated problem in the arithmetic book. If some students felt superior to others in the one-room schools, such feelings were rarely verbalized. However, I do recall that at the Monroe County school I first attended, some of us would taunt a family of poverty-ridden brothers and sisters by singing a ditty in which their father was supposedly speaking to their mother:

> The pond's on fire,
> The spring's gone dry;
> Oh, me, Bessie,
> Are you gonna let me lay here and die?

Although the educational facilities were often crude, community members nonetheless took pride in the school, a feeling undergirded by the belief that learning makes a better person. The one-room school was not only a place to learn reading, writing, and arithmetic but an institution that fostered socialization, cooperation, and discipline, both in the schoolroom and on the playground.

Many of the schools in the Upper Cumberland, governed by a board of trustees, displayed rules of discipline in one corner of the blackboard. Penalties for breaking rules were upheld by the teacher who, in most cases, tried only to maintain an atmosphere appropriate for learning. Early teachers often sat "while hearing recitations, with a long beech or hickory switch in their hands," wrote the itinerant Methodist minister, A. B. Wright, about the discipline meted out in Tennessee's Upper Cumberland around 1840. "The severity of the lash, or the number," he

Children in a Clay County one-room school, mid-1930s (Photo courtesy of Landon Anderson)

continued, "was according to the severity of the offense committed." Such whippings were common, but so were other forms of punishment, which might require that a child stay in at recess, stand in a corner, stand with one arm raised until it felt as if it were going to fall off, sit on the dunce's stool, shake hands with the opposition, or read aloud to the entire school a love note that had been intercepted and handed to the teacher.

The early one-room schools, both free and subscription, were simple log structures fashioned with small windows and puncheon or rough-sawn planks for flooring. Student seats were made out of round logs split in the center and hewn smooth with a broad ax. In the more isolated areas of the Upper Cumberland, schools such as these were still in existence in the early twentieth century, although the split log seats gave way long ago to homemade desks.

Judge J. W. Wells of Cumberland County, Kentucky, described the seating in the Cumberland and Russell county schools he attended during the mid- to late 1880s:

The appliances or things used in the old-time schools I attended were rare and simple. The most inconvenient things of all were the seating fixtures. What we had to sit upon for hours at a time were split logs made of small trees from six to eight inches in diameter with the split sides turned up and supported on four legs made of smaller bushes. These seats had neither backs nor footrests, and stood about two feet above the floor which made it very tiresome for small pupils to sit during the long hours of study with their feet dangling in the air. Children were required to place their books and slates on their seats by their right sides so they would always know where to reach to get them. With a wriggling lad on every side of you it was difficult to keep your curriculum adjusted. Slates were used altogether then to write and "cypher" on. It was years before I saw a tablet in school. I remember an industrious little fellow having to spend thirty minutes on the stool behind the door in paying his penalty for having drawn the picture of a pig with a curly tail on his slate and showing it to his benchmate. Nothing was permissible on the slates but writing or figures.

Arnold Watson, also of Cumberland County, explained why the slate boards and slate pencils used by students in some schools as late as 1940 were unsanitary. "Most of the kids spit on their hand or spit on their sleeve and rubbed their writing off the slate that way," he recalled. "They often did their problem solving and composition assignments at the blackboard, at least after the latter devices came along." Before the advent of these slick-surfaced wonders, however, teachers often had a makeshift "black board" fashioned from native timbers. Judge Wells described them:

Sometimes a friend would dress three wide poplar planks and dye them black on one side, nail them to two legs and lean them against the wall of the building and call it teacher's blackboard. The children were not permitted to use it in any way. He would set a small wooden box in the loft full of something he called chalk. Occasionally he would reach up and get a small stick and write on his blackboard. This amused all of us kids very much and of course, kid-like, all of us had an anxiety to get hold of some of it but every time he wrote a little he would place the balance in his box which we could not reach. So one day when we caught him away from the room we caucused to satisfy our curiosity. Some boys were placed at the door and some at the window as sentinels, while one lad scaled the wall and handed the box down to another boy. We all looked and examined it thoroughly, going far enough as to smell and taste it, but dared not make a mark either on the board or on the wall.

That was the only time that term we felt of chalk.

In more progressive and populous communities in the region, educational facilities were improved and updated throughout the late nineteenth and early twentieth centuries. The school term lasted any-where from ten weeks to five months, usually beginning in July, until about 1921 when school systems began gradually extending the school year to the present-day nine months. Local historians and others who drew upon traditional information provided a storehouse of material about the typical one-room school as it existed from 1890 through the mid-twentieth century. The Reverend C. L. Holt of Overton County offered the following account:

> Most all the school houses were frame with one room. Of course there were some school buildings made of brick or stone with several rooms in towns or larger communities. These buildings were heated with wood or coal stoves which were usually located near the center of the room. It was difficult to heat these rooms during the coldest days of winter. Drinking water was carried from a near-by spring or drawn from a well with a chain and pulley. During the hot season two boys were sent with one or two buckets, each of which held about ten quarts. Girls were rarely ever permitted to carry water. All pupils drank from a common dipper until teachers learned more safe methods of using the individual drinking cups.

Walter B. Overton's 1927 master's thesis on Jackson County schools notes that the county had sixty school buildings that year, fifty-four of which had daily drinking water stored in buckets. Students at fifty-two of the sixty schools shared a common drinking cup. Given a similar situation across the Upper Cumberland, it is little wonder that children's diseases spread so rapidly, in spite of the universal asafetida (a bad-smelling gum resin used to repel disease) bag worn by numerous children well into the twentieth century.

Toilet facilities at one-room schools in the Upper Cumberland were minimal. It was not uncommon for the boys to use one thicket, or large rock, or gulley, and the girls to use another. At some schools crude privies were constructed behind the building, but this was not common until the late 1920s. These structures were invariably targeted by groups of local boys and girls who, on Halloween night, would return to the school grounds, lift one (or both) of the privies from its foundation and stick it, roof first, into the toilet hole.

Over the entire area the time spent inside the schoolroom studying was called *books*; the two short breaks were called *recesses*, and the longer period at noon was called *dinner time*. Occasionally the term *playtime* was applied to the three breaks. *Books and playtime*, then, meant school, just as *sugar and coffee* meant items bought at the store.

The school day usually began at eight o'clock with the ringing of the hand bell. This time-honored method of calling children to "take up books" lasted in most one-room schools until they ceased to exist in the region. The students, having walked or ridden horses upward of three miles to be present, entered the building and sat down, boys on one side

of the room and girls on the other. Such interior segregation along gender lines was the rule rather than the exception during the nineteenth century; it sometimes meant two separate playgrounds as well.

Usually, the teacher or one of the pupils read a short Bible passage and said a prayer. The student body then sang a song or two before students were called to the front of the room by individual classes to recite their lessons and obtain new assignments.

Each class lasted about fifteen minutes. Students not in class were preparing their lessons, listening to the class in session, or planning some type of mischief, of which there was plenty in a room filled with sixty or more students. The activities of the morning were broken by a thirty-minute recess, after which classes resumed until lunchtime when school was dismissed for one hour. A fifteen-minute afternoon recess allowed for a short period of diversion, and school was officially dismissed about three o'clock. Students then began their walk home, empty lunch containers in hand.

Boys and girls in a basketball game at Hidalgo in southern Wayne County, late 1920s (Photo courtesy of Hattie Edwards)

Lunches, which were carried to school in metal lard buckets or syrup pails (with their metal lids tightly closed, these containers served as fireless cookers that blended all the foods' flavors by lunchtime), usually consisted of cornbread, biscuits, corn, beans, tomatoes, or fried potato sandwiches. One Monroe County family of five brothers and sisters had nothing but a quart of sorghum molasses and several cold biscuits each day during the depression years of the late 1930s. If corn were in season, it was not unusual for the wet cobs to fly through the air and hit unsuspecting classmates on the back or head.

Lunchtime was a special time for children attending the one-room school, as they had ample time to eat and to engage in play. Students typically ate outside the building under a shade tree; during these times there was often rapid exchange of food. Mary Cummings of Gainesboro, who recalled trading biscuits for cornbread at school, also described the unappealing appearance of many items of food brought by the children:

My father had a gristmill in which he ground wheat and corn. And our biscuits, I guess, were awfully good. But I didn't think they were good because they were dark colored.

Well, we would take a hot biscuit and butter it and put brown sugar on it and fold it together so the sugar would melt into the biscuit. And we'd take that to school and swap it to the neighbor's children for cornbread. And we'd crumble that cornbread in a bowl of molasses and butter and mix it up and everybody ate out of the same little bowl. Of course each one had our own spoon! And we'd pass that around until we had the bowl licked out.

Our dinner otherwise was usually vegetables in season, like corn or beans, tomatoes, whatever they might have. And when the fresh vegetables were gone, they boiled potatoes. And I can recall some children bringing biscuit and fried potato sandwiches. The biscuits weren't even brown, and neither were the potatoes! They were the most tasteless-looking things I ever saw. But these were healthy boys and they grew into husky men, so I guess it was all right.

During morning recess and lunch break, students engaged in vigorous playtime activities that diverted them from the regimen of study. Such activities were voluntary, competitive, and nonproductive, existing outside the realms of routine reality. All such folk games and recreational forms were and still are passed along by word of mouth and through imitation from one time and place to another. Generally of unknown origin, the games' rules are often changed in minor ways.

One of the most demanding and dangerous forms of play involved both boys and girls scrambling up trees and through the tops, jumping from one tree to another. The objective was to reach the next one without falling. In one popular version, a child would climb to the top of a thin sapling, make it rock to and fro, then leap from it while in forward motion and land in the cushion-like branches of a cedar tree farther down the slope. Sometimes the strategy did not work and children landed on the ground; if they were lucky, they could get up and walk away unhurt.

Fox and the hounds was a game of strategy that took children far away from the schoolhouse. The fox, generally a long-legged older male student, was pursued by a pack of hounds (the other players). He was sometimes so clever that by doubling back across his own trail time and again he successfully eluded the pack for an entire afternoon. When this occurred, both the fox and the hounds were subsequently punished by the teacher.

Another game of strategy was marbles, a favorite playground pastime at most of the one-room schools along the upper reaches of the Cumberland, especially in Jackson, Clay, Monroe, Cumberland, and Adair counties. Most children saved their pennies so they could purchase agate marbles, which they guarded carefully on the marble yard. However, young boys (as well as older men) in the Cumberland River counties made their own marbles. This complicated process (described more fully in the final chapter) took almost two weeks to complete.

All forms of ball games, as well as numerous other games such as mumblety peg; stink base; Patti, Patti, sheep meat; crack the whip; and shinney involved physical skill and dexterity. One particular form of ball play, commonly known as town ball, preceded baseball in the region and was popular at many of the one-room schools. The balls used in the game were handmade, fashioned from worn socks. In early times, the boys took homemade yarn socks and unraveled them to make balls; in later years balls of white string were used. They whittled out their own bats and board-like paddles with which to hit the ball.

In town ball, which went by various names, sides were chosen; then the two leaders spit on one side of the paddle and threw it into the air. If a leader called "wet" and the wet side was up, that side would be "in town" and would play a round until each player had batted out. The ball was pitched with an underarm delivery to each batter. If the batter missed three times and the ball was caught behind on the third miss he or she was out; if the batter hit a ball and it was caught before all four bases had been successfully circled, the runner was out. Base runners could be crossed out between bases if the ball was thrown across their path.

Other school games that called for the use of a ball included cat ball (often called bat ball) and bullpen. Cat ball was a modified game of tennis that was played without a net. Two batters faced each other and swatted the ball back and forth between them.

Bullpen was a rough game, which only the larger boys played. Former school superintendent Ira Bell of Wayne County described it:

A circle was drawn in the yard with a diameter the length of the shoes that the boy wore, his heels against one side of the circumference and his toes right across on the other; and they chose one to put into the bullpen and the big boys about thirty feet away would take three throws of that ball at the fellow in the bullpen; and he had to keep his feet within the circle; and if he was able to dodge the ball three times without being hit, he came out of the circle. The one that missed him three times went into the circle and was "it."

Other common games involving skill and dexterity included jump rope and antny over. Jumping the rope was popular everywhere, whether the rope was a plowline brought from home or a long, slender grapevine obtained in the woods. Boys and girls alike lined up and ran into and out of the path of the swinging rope. Anyone who hesitated and watched the rope coming down without jumping in was "catching flies." "Hot pepper" was the name used when the rope was thrown very rapidly and "high water" when it was thrown several inches above the ground. Sometimes two or more children would jump at the same time and even have small individual ropes to jump as they bounded over the long rope. Ordinarily, single rope-jumping was accompanied by rhymes, of which there must be hundreds throughout the United States. They are still being created; I hear of new ones almost every year, often slanted toward some recent national or world event.

The game that everybody knew was Antny over (also called Annie and even Anthony over). Equal teams occupied opposite sides of the schoolhouse. The team with the ball called, "Antny"; the other team replied, "Over." The first one to say, "Here it comes," threw the ball and started running around to the other side of the building, team members streaming along behind. The side with the ball tried to touch or hit as many members of the opposing team as possible; those so hit became members of that team. On it went, until one side got all or most of the players.

Patti, Patti, sheep meat was "as rough as football," according to Lynnie White of Monticello, "and we [boys and girls] charged each other just as hard. The teacher usually stopped this game after we had torn enough clothes off each other." Equally rough were cracking the whip, a game in which the "whip" (a student at the end of the line) could "get slung a mile and maybe hurt," and shinney, a game described by White "as a forerunner of hockey, except we played it with tin cans and sprouts with roots at the end of them."

A guessing game or pantomime of universal appeal here as elsewhere was called going to New York, going to New Orleans, or something similar. In this game, each of two groups of players had its home base. A line called 'the enemy line" was drawn to separate the two opposing groups. Players in one of the groups decided among themselves what to act out when they approached the line. This done, they went to the line and were asked by the enemy group, "Where are you going?"

"Going to New York."

"What's your trade?"

"Lemonade, made in the shade, stirred with a spade."

"Well, get to work and get it made."

Each member of the visiting group began at this point to pantomime some agreed-upon task; providing the enemy with the task's initial. Thus "switw" stood for "sawing wood in the woods." Once the enemy correctly identified the activity, all the players on the visiting team ran for home base, with the enemy close on their heels. Those caught were taken back to the enemy base. The game continued until all members of one group were captured by the other team.

Small children played drop the handkerchief or ring around the rosie. Some teachers are remembered because they would play these games, such as I spy (or hide 'n seek), with even the smallest boys and girls. If the schoolhouse were in the woods, there was always a seasonal interest in building and furnishing playhouses—a non-game activity—where little girls emulated their mothers and other women of the community. Their playhouses were usually constructed under the shade of large trees. They gathered moss, covering rocks with it for beds and chairs, and used forked sticks for people. Acorn cups, or broken bits of pottery found around every household became dishes. Anything edible or something purely imaginary could be served for food. Every girl was hostess of her own house and had her own family. She could invite people to come and see her and feed them dinner or supper.

When children tired of their games, they often amused themselves by gathering chestnuts or walnuts and cracking them. Older boys and girls often parched corn over small earthen furnaces covered by pieces of tin roofing. The corn was poured onto the top of the hot tin; when it was parched, the students ate the hot corn and shared with those around them.

Friday afternoon in the one-room school was a celebrated time of the week, when special academic activities provided competition and entertainment, both for students and for members of the community who wished to attend. In early years, spelling bees and later on railroad spellings and ciphering matches (rapid calculation at the blackboard) were the most popular of the Friday events. All students participated in them.

In railroad spelling, the person who began the game was required to spell r-a-i-l-r-o-a-d. The next in line, who had to spell a word that began with the last letter in the previous word, invariably spelled d-a-n-d-y.

The race was on! The third person had to spell a word beginning with the letter "y," and so on down the line. All who spelled their words incorrectly had to return to their desks. The ultimate winner was often awarded a prize for being the best speller in school.

Speeches, recitations, and plays were also common Friday events, providing an opportunity for students to perform in front of an audience and allowing them to overcome the fears often associated with such an experience.

Pie and box suppers held in the school for the entire community promoted a sense of unity and cooperation. These suppers, held mainly in the Upland South from around 1890 until the early 1950s, were community functions that raised money for the school. Each single young female in the community prepared a "box" decorated with crepe paper and ribbons and containing a pie or enough food for herself and one other. The boxes were auctioned off to the highest male bidder who assumed the privilege of eating with the girl who had prepared the box. The identity of the box's owner was a presumed secret, but usually the girl's name "leaked out." Her male suitor was expected to buy her box during open bidding. Sometimes, however, a rival would "run her box up" on the suitor, or a gang of fellows would pool their money and outstrip all bidders. Fights often ensued between suitors and, if they were from different communities, between communities as well.

Music was a common feature at such social gatherings, performed by local stringbands whose members are often still legendary in their respective communities.

Through such activities the one-room schools served crucial roles as bonding agents in the community. Students were made aware of a sense of family and community and of belonging to something that was solid and enduring. Whatever different religious and political views were held by parents, their children all went to the same school. Often, these youngsters were taught by the same educator who had taught their parents. It was not uncommon for pre–World War II grandparents, children, and grandchildren to share fond recollections of sitting under the same tree or on the same stump or large, protruding tree roots while eating lunches brought from home in white oak or willow baskets or in lard buckets.

All students who attended one-room schools did not necessarily learn their lessons well and become scholars or prominent leaders in adult life. But few children who attended a one-room school for any length of time came away without having gained respect for other people and acquired social skills important for success in the community. Despite its handicaps, the one-room school in the Upper Cumberland, as elsewhere, provided an education that left its imprint on generations of people. It continued as a force in the region into the 1950s and its image is permanently imprinted in the minds of area residents who recall with fondness their years spent there.

At present there are no one-room schools in the Upper Cumberland; they generally ceased to exist during the 1950s and early 1960s as a result of school consolidation measures. Historian David Tyack, writing in *The One Best System*, describes increased state and federal intervention into these community-based school systems, so that there was more outside control over them. Such schools were seen as antiquated, he writes, staffed by poorly trained teachers, conducted in less than adequate buildings, and poorly attended, all of which were considered to be problems that had to be overcome. On the other hand, he points out, these community schools were institutions in which "the child acquired his values and skills from his family and from neighbors of all ages and conditions." Furthermore, the teachers were products of their own schools, the community used the school for a variety of social functions, and younger students could look to older students as role models. Indeed there were problems at times with quality of instruction, attendance, and health conditions, but these were community matters and served as unifying challenges for local residents.

With consolidation, these historic entities were incorporated into larger elementary and middle schools that were constructed with state and federal monies, along with newly imposed local taxes. Consolidation also became possible because of the advent of modern transportation, which, while lessening distances, also weakened the bonds of community previously existing in small towns, villages, and rural settlements. Students who had walked to school over dirt roads and trails now stood alongside newly paved arteries to await the arrival of the school bus that would transport them to some other educational center miles away.

"Many of the older members of each community still mourn the loss of their school," writes Patricia G. Lane, author of *Mountain View*. These people feel that "close relationships began to break down when improving the community school ceased to unite residents for a common goal." A resident of the Mountain View community, located in Cumberland County, Tennessee, commented, "I thought losing the school was just about the worst thing that ever happened. When you lose your school, you lose your close community."

RELIGION AND THE COMMUNITY

The haste with which people moved westward during pioneer times generally precluded their bringing along organized religion. It was more expedient to lay aside church matters for awhile. Nonetheless, many of these frontier people were devout Christians and held religious meetings in their homes and at convenient outdoor locations.

Religion was soon to become an important force in the culture of the Upper Cumberland. Presbyterian, Baptist, and Methodist preachers represented the earliest denominations to bring organized religion to the area. The Presbyterians may have been first of all through their role in the revival movement that swept across the region in the form of camp meetings beginning about 1800. However, the nature of Presbyterian centralism and its demand for a trained ministry led to the emergence of Baptist and Methodist churches, and soon thereafter the Church of Christ, as the most popular with people in the Upper Cumberland. In contrast to the Presbyterians' demand for an educated clergy, Baptists felt that their preachers were "called by God" and that He would empower them with the ability to read the Bible and preach. Methodists were much like Baptists in this regard, although they did require that their circuit riders be able to read.

Professor Homer Kemp of Cookeville writes of the humorous consequences of these lax educational standards:

Well into the nineteenth century, the old-time country preachers regularly denounced "book larnin" from the pulpit and quite often could not read. They cited sermon texts from the Bible from memory, a faulty memory at that. It was quite common for a preacher to cite his text as "somewhere betwixt the lids of the goodbook."

As late as the late years of the nineteenth century, F. D. Srygley, in his *Seventy Years in Dixie*, wrote of witnessing sermons preached on such "Biblical" texts as "make hay while the sun shines" and "every tub should stand on its own bottom." There are hundreds of tales about comic misquotations of texts and mispronunciation of words—with a resulting twist of scriptural meaning.

The ability of the Baptists and Methodists to adapt to the necessities of a demanding frontier environment contributed to the strength of these denominations during those early years when the church was truly the center of social as well as religious life. John Wesley's plan of rotating ministers adapted well to the Upper Cumberland. Bishop Francis Asbury, charged with the responsibility of carrying Methodism to the newly settled land, elaborated on Wesley's original scheme by setting up a system of regular circuits. The Cumberland Circuit was organized in 1787.

The circuit riders were assigned a route along which they preached at regular intervals. Additionally, as they rode from church to church, they preached wherever they found a willing audience, be it a church, barn, house, brush arbor, or under a large shade tree. There were few areas too remote for these dedicated preachers to reach.

It is said that Isaac Woodard, one of the early circuit-riding ministers, divided his sermons into three verbal assaults. He attacked Presbyterians, Baptists, and the sissyfied, weak-kneed Methodist ministers. He once railed against a Presbyterian deacon who "cheated his neighbor out of a horse, then went to prayer meeting and prayed for his neighbor's conversion." Another time Woodard reputedly remarked, "Some Methodist preachers are like Si Dugan's old red steer. They make noise enough to pull the world, but not a pound will they pull."

Such apocryphal stories were also told on Baptist ministers. Kemp writes that a hard-shell Baptist preacher compared the three Protestant denominations in one of his famous sermons. The "Piscapalians are a highfalutin' lot who are much like the turkey buzzard that flies high into the sky and then rushes down to feed on the carcass of a dead hoss." Since the Methodists believe in degrees of grace until they finally achieve perfection, he said, they are like a squirrel that goes way up into a tree, jumps from branch to branch, and finally falls to the ground—just as Methodists fall from grace. Baptists on the other hand believe in "once saved always saved," thus resembling the possum that can hang by its tail in a persimmon tree through thunder and earthquakes. "You can shake one foot loose," the Baptist preacher claimed, "but the other'n is there. And you can shake all feet loose, but he just laps his tail around the limb and hangs on forever."

Denominational folk customs, some humorous, some solemn and beautiful, have been followed through the years until many of them have become dogma. It was fairly typical until the 1930s for some congregations to hold church business meetings on the Saturday before their monthly preaching on Sunday. Some of the region's more fundamental groups are still "ruled by Saturday." For example, they might hold preaching services on the Sunday following the third Saturday. During some months, this particular Sunday may be the fourth one that month, but it follows the third Saturday. No one knows where this practice originated, but it is still done because "that's the way we've always done it in our church."

Congregational prayers as observed in the more fundamentalist churches are just that—prayers said aloud in unison by the congregation. The more saintly church members gather in the altar area to invoke God's presence and blessings on the assembled group. The prayer may be for a sick church member, a wayward person, an unsaved sinner, or a much-needed rain. Someone is always singled out to lead the prayer, but all of those gathered in the altar area pray aloud in unison. One by one, the people finish their individual prayers and the group falls quiet as only the voice of the one called on to lead the prayer can still be heard. When the "amens" are all said, the group breaks into song—usually one of praise or thanksgiving—and a round of handshaking and tearful embraces follows.

Many humorous traditional stories are told about the prayers offered up by clergy and laypersons alike. Some of these stories have made the rounds from generation to generation and from one denomination to another. Bud Robinson, an early evangelist from White County, is said to have traveled two hundred thousand miles, preached thirty-three thousand times, and witnessed to one hundred thousand people at the altar during his revivals. The following prayer is attributed to him:

Lord, give me a backbone as big as a saw log, and ribs like the sleepers under the church floor; put iron shoes on me, and galvanized breeches. And give me a rhinoceros' hide for a skin, and hang a wagon load of determination up in the gable end of my soul, and help me to sign the contract to fight the devil as long as I've got a fist, and bite him as long as I've got a tooth, and then gum him 'til I die. All this I ask for Christ's sake. Amen!

In the Skaggs Creek Baptist Church of north central Monroe County, it was almost ritual for those called upon to pray aloud to thank the Lord for "allowing us to gather once again on this old hilltop." On one occasion, a somewhat nervous deacon began his prayer with the words, "Now, Lord, we have gathered once more on this old housetop. . . ."

Hazel Montell enjoys recounting the traditional story about the time some of the Skaggs Creek members had gathered for a special session of prayer for much-needed rain. Just before the prayer was scheduled to begin, Preacher Joe Miller rode up, dismounted, and broke up the prayer meeting with the pronouncement, "There's no need to pray. It's not going to a bit of good as long as the damn wind's blowing out of the east."

Mel Tharp of Crossville recorded an amusing story about the time a needy resident of Silver Point was instructed by the preacher to ask the Lord for help:

I reckon this happened sometime right after the First World War. They was a feller living over around Silver Point and him and his family were just about on starvation. The preacher got some good folks together one night and went over to the fellow's house to see if maybe a little praying would help.

Now this was a good man but he was sort of bad to cuss. The preacher told the man to get down on his knees and let the Lord know what he needed. So the feller got down and started to pray: "Oh Lord, could you please send me a barrel of flour? And Lord I need a barrel of salt. Lord please send me a barrel of pepper, too."

Suddenly, the man stopped praying, slapped his leg and shouted, "Oh hell! That's too much pepper!"

The means of salvation is a subject that has caused a great deal of controversy and passionate expression over the years. While some denominations hold that one cannot know until death occurs whether heaven or hell will be the final abode, most teach that it is possible to know in the here and now about eternity. One is "saved" by exercising proper faith. In most early churches, salvation was sought either at the altar or at the mourner's bench, as it was generally called. Sometimes called the "anxious seat," this particular pew is located near the pulpit. It is here that the sinner goes to repent, pray, and wait for salvation, head buried all the while on an arm folded across the back of the pew. It is generally felt that this process of "praying one's way through to salvation" takes from seven to ten days. When salvation comes, the seeker sits erect on the mourner's bench, either crying from joy or smiling, thus announcing to others present what has happened.

Some churches still use the mourner's bench and still hold to the lengthy period for obtaining salvation. These churches, not always rural, are critical of the "big city churches" and certain progressive rural churches, labeling them as "modernists." It is not uncommon to see signs along the road, or in front of the churches themselves, that announce the practice of an "Old Fashion Plan of Salvation" or "Altar-Centered Religion."

In some churches, new converts customarily make a public declaration of their salvation and are required to relate their experience in a persuasive manner in front of the entire congregation as a prerequisite for baptism and acceptance into the church fellowship. In earlier years, immersion usually took place in ponds, rivers, or creeks, often in the icy November chill. Numerous people enjoy recounting their experience of being baptized in water that was frozen over at the time so that the ice had to be removed before the ritual could take place.

Outdoor baptism is still widely practiced, although most city churches now have built-in pools. Opinions vary as to which of the two is the more appropriate. An apocryphal story holds that the membership in a Pulaski County church split over this issue a few years back, with two separate churches resulting, one called "hot water Baptists" and the other "cold water Baptists."

Shouting by one or many was a common part of pre–World War II religious services. This display of ecstatic emotion (shouting, screaming, crying, waving of arms) could take place at any time, but it typically occurred during another person's testimony of God's abundant grace or while the congregation was engaged in song. I witnessed a few people shouting during the years 1985 to 1990 as I went from church to church documenting gospel music in Kentucky's Upper Cumberland. By and large, however, people no longer shout. The demise of this phenomenon is attributable to the emergence of an educated clergy in both rural and urban churches. An elderly devout woman in Tompkinsville, known for a lifetime of shouting at the drop of a hat, was asked in the late 1960s why she no longer did so at church. "Well, I'm as close to God now as I ever was," she responded, "but since the new pastor don't believe in shouting, the Lord just doesn't lead me to do it any more."

Until recent years, Baptists held that children do not reach the "age of accountability" for sins committed until they are thirteen or fourteen years old. Because of this rather formal position, children were taught not to seek salvation until their early teen years. Too, most religious denominations in the region believe that if a child dies before reaching the age of accountability, his or her soul will go on to heaven. A beautiful illustration of this belief was penned by the Reverend A. B. Wright, famous in the Upper Cumberland as a nineteenth-century Methodist circuit rider. Wright's diary entry reads: "In the fall of the year our babe was greatly troubled in teething, that led to inflammation of the brain. On a fair golden autumn day—September 13, 1858—about one o'clock in the afternoon, he plumed his angel wings, and with a smile bid farewell to a sin cursed world, and flew home to glory."

Many people waited until they were forty or older to join the church. Their public statements of faith and conversion, which were often dramatic, were frequently retold by others in the church in the same fashion that contemporary historical legends are transmitted orally. Especially important in this regard are "death-bed conversion" stories. People seem to enjoy recounting episodes of miraculous salvation experienced just before someone drew his or her last breath. Invariably, someone will be overheard to mutter, "Yes, but he sure didn't have the time to build up any rewards to enjoy in heaven."

A minister's delivery of a sermon varies from individual to individual and from denomination to denomination. However, spiritual preaching, or preaching that depends solely on inspiration, is still in evidence and in the past was very widespread. The Reverend Gifford Walters of Monticello, a retired Baptist minister, told of preachers who once spoke with a hand over one ear so as to allow the Holy Spirit to enter through the other ear and have no means of escape except through the mouth. Such deliveries were usually high-pitched and resembled chanting. They were not unlike the sounds made by an auctioneer or a southern politician stumping for local office. Sermons delivered in this manner build up the emotional levels of both preacher and listeners.

Folklorist Bruce Rosenberg comments on the distinction between "manuscript" and "spiritual" preachers. The manuscript preacher works from a prepared text, while the spiritual preacher shares a sermon that is "inspired"; that is, the preacher steps up to the pulpit and is fed directly by God. Even inspired sermons, says Rosenberg, entail a certain amount of basic preparation a few days before delivery, but the minister waits for the final words to come spontaneously when he stands before the congregation. For the spiritual preacher the moment of real sermon composition occurs in the actual performance itself. Perhaps the basic outline or theme is fixed in the preacher's mind, but the content fluctuates, following no strict pattern. Certain traditional phrases or expressions are called into use by both pastor and listeners throughout the sermon: "Thank you, Jesus," "Praise God," "Praise the Lord," "the Christ of the Bible," and "amen" are typical examples. A local witticism holds that "saying amen to a preacher is like saying sic'um to a dog. The more you say it, the more they'll do it."

Local radio stations have been natural outlets for this type of preaching. While the practice is not as common as it was during the 1940s and 1950s, many stations across the region still broadcast highly charged emotional sermons, preceded by string band gospel music groups performing such songs as "After I Leave for Worlds Unknown, What Will I Leave Behind," and "I've Got More to Go to Heaven for Than I Had Yesterday." Often the preacher uses the chanting style of delivery, punctuating the sermon by the frequent utterance of the word "uh," even when asking for contributions: "These programs uh do cost money uh praise the Lord uh that's pretty high preaching uh and singing uh praise the Lord!"

Spiritual preachers were at one time in the majority in the Upper Cumberland. A widespread story tells of a young man who felt that he, too, was being called into the ministry. According to custom, he prayed and asked God for some kind of positive sign. When he saw the letters "GPC" written across the sky, he interpreted them to mean "Go Preach Christ." After two or three of his efforts at preaching failed miserably, an old but progressive deacon of the church asked, "Son, did it ever occur to you that the letters 'GPC' might mean 'Go Plow Corn'?"

A strong tradition, and one that is still practiced in some area churches, was that of separating men and women during religious services. Men sat on one side of the sanctuary, women and small children on the other. Those couples that preferred to remain together typically sat on the women's side or in the middle section of pews if the church had three rows of benches. A dozen or so men sat in a select group of pews located to the right of the pulpit and boosted the preacher with words and utterances that emphasized points made in the sermon. This was called the "amen corner." In some churches, including my childhood church, certain women sat on the other side of the pulpit opposite the men. This section was jokingly referred to as the "awomen corner."

It was possibly in order to strengthen the concept of gender segregation at church that many of the buildings were built with two front doors, presumably one for the men and one for the women. No one knows for sure whether this was really the situation, or whether the two doors served some other function. In any case, new churches today have only one front door.

At many churches throughout the Upper Cumberland it was once common practice, and still is to some extent, for men and older boys— and sometimes women—to remain outside the meeting house during religious services. This custom reflects the important social role the church played in the local community. These fellows discussed crops, politics, and other issues of the day while seated on the backs of their legs and heels. This position is referred to as "hunkering down" and could be maintained for long periods of time. Sometimes those present whittled as they chatted.

Methods of paying preachers for services rendered varied over the years. During frontier years, when it was difficult to ship corn back east across the mountains and impossible to ship it down the Mississippi because the Spanish controlled the port at New Orleans, the corn was often converted into whiskey. It was not uncommon for preachers to be paid for a year's work with eight to ten barrels of whiskey. Guaranteed salaries for ministers were unusual until after the Civil War, and then only urban churches participated. Rural church ministers were randomly paid by individual church members until World War II. The Reverend J. A. Smithwick of the Sand Lick community in Monroe County received only a pair of knit socks in payment for an entire year of preaching in 1868. I have personally witnessed church members secretly pass currency or silver to the minister as they shook hands with him at the end of a service.

Revivals have always played a large role in the religious life of the Upper Cumberland. Camp meetings served as the chief revival tool throughout the nineteenth century and well into the twentieth century in some instances. The camp meetings were eventually replaced by annual revivals of two weeks' duration. These in turn gave way to biannual revivals of a week to ten days' duration beginning generally in the 1950s when more and more rural churches achieved full-time status.

Throughout much of the nineteenth century, the entire community attended revivals in the various churches, since less attention was paid then to denominational differences. The fact that revivals served as social functions helped to account for their popularity from frontier days through the 1930s. Church was the chief place to meet old friends and make new acquaintances, especially those of the opposite gender, and to tease or aggravate persons seated on the inside. It was common practice for the teen-age boys, who remained on the outside during the religious services, to toss pebbles and dogwood berries through the open windows at certain persons inside. A widespread story holds that some "extra-mean fellows" actually tossed a cat through a small window behind the pulpit onto the preacher's back. The favorite targets of all, however, were the young, eligible females.

At the close of revival services each night, boys and girls of courting age walked together down the road home. Sometimes a grown fellow who had ridden horseback would ask a special girl to ride double with him, sitting in the saddle while he rode bareback behind her. Naturally, his arms had to reach around her waist so that he could effectively hold the reins and steer the horse down the road!

Like the revival meetings, annual Baptist associational meetings were social as well as religious events. These gatherings brought together delegates from Baptist churches that were associated with each other because of geographical proximity and doctrine. Thus, Free Will Baptists, General Baptists, Missionary Baptists, Separate Baptists, Southern Baptists, United Baptists, and other Baptist denominations in the Upper Cumberland held annual "'sosational" meetings. Beatrice Powell of Russell Springs writes that the association meetings were used as reference points in the community, with people marking certain events as happening during the sessions. Many young couples set their wedding dates to coincide with them.

These meetings usually lasted about three days and two nights. People in attendance stayed as guests in the homes of associational members living near the host church or campgrounds. Springhouses were often built especially to refrigerate the food brought along by the visitors. Stacks of hay and oats, as well as full cribs of corn, were set aside for the horses.

Services during the day were characterized by lengthy sermons, statistical reports from the various churches, singing, and praying. Testimonials of prayer and faith were heard during these sessions, especially at night. Spiritual preaching often prompted spontaneous shouting and singing.

The behavior of those present was not always completely pious. There was noisemaking in the adjacent woods, including rowdy behavior, pistol shots, and animals being verbally attacked. Inside the building, crying children were often slapped and told to hush up. And people were always milling around the two or three concession stands that featured cold drinks, hot dogs, and ice cream.

Personal behavior of individual church members, at home and in public, was carefully scrutinized by all churches in the Upper Cumberland. One's personal appearance was a matter of concern as well; in earlier times, women who bobbed their hair or wore lipstick were often the topic of criticism from the pulpit. People were seldom "churched" (removed from the church rolls) for these offences. They were, however, excluded for immoral reasons, including "lying out all night with a man in a thick settlement," "communing with other denominations," "taking part in shooting matches," "failure to attend church services," "not paying debts," "producing an illegitimate child," and for attending horseraces, dancing, drinking, or committing adultery. Nowadays, exclusion from a church rarely occurs. When it does, it is usually because the offender has "joined a church of another faith and order."

Custodial care of church buildings used to be up to members of the congregation and still is in most rural areas. Today, most buildings have central heating and cooling and indoor plumbing, but that was not always the case. Families at one time took turns heating the church, preparing for the communion, and seeing to it that the communal water bucket and the preacher's private pitcher were filled before the scheduled service. Water was taken from the bucket with a tin or enamel dipper that was then placed back in the bucket. A few children and fearless adults might tiptoe to the bucket for a sip of water at various times during the lengthy sermon.

Church attendance usually meant "a good dinner, visiting with friends, watching the pretty girls [or good-looking boys], courting a little and hearing a fire and brimstone sermon." Rural dwellers did not see distant neighbors very often; thus "meeting day" was a special event. The church, along with the community school, was truly the center of one's social existence in the days before the automobile.

Old-time preachers never thought of retiring or leaving the ministry until death took them from their earthly labors. Their simple philosophy was, "I want to be in the field when the sun goes down." The Reverend J. H. Swann of Tompkinsville (formerly of Willette, Tennessee) celebrated his eighty-fifth birthday in 1958. Numerous friends gathered at the Tompkinsville Baptist Church to pay tribute. Through tear-filled eyes he thanked his friends in a quivering voice and then commented that a younger preacher friend had recently said to him, "I've been preaching for thirty years and I am tired."

The reverend claimed that he responded half sarcastically, "I've been preaching sixty-six years and I ain't tired yet." Swann lived to be ninety-six.

Song leaders are almost as legendary as some of the old preachers. Coyle Copeland of Crawford, Overton County, recalled the time his songleading great-grandfather nipped too heavily at a jar of moonshine whiskey:

I'll tell you a good one on him. Back then only a few people could read and write. People would get a letter and get on a mule and travel seven-eight miles to get somebody to read the letter for them—and to answer the letter. Actually, there were only four-five people down in that area that could read and write. He happened to be one of them.

He was a j. p. [justice of the peace], and he was also a singer. He'd lead singing at church. And he could pray as loud and as long as anybody could. And if he's like the rest of them, he probably took up collection, too!

Well, they told it on him that they got him to agree to come over to this brush harbor meeting and lead singing. Used to have a lot of these brush harbor meetings. He was to go over and be there on a certain night.

On the way he fell in with some evil companions. He found some fellows making whiskey, so the old man got drunk and stayed there with them four days. And they had to put the meeting off for four days to let the old man sober up.

We are not told whether the old fellow was to lead the congregation in shape-note singing or line out the hymns for them. The once widespread practice of lining out hymns has apparently vanished in the Upper Cumberland. Illiteracy or a lack of songbooks, or both, spawned this method of singing. The practice consisted of the song leader calling out one or two lines of a hymn and the congregation responding by repeating the lines.

Many such religious gatherings were held outdoors or in schoolhouses, as church buildings were not found in every community during early times. This was still true at the beginning of the twentieth century. Albert Bilbrey of Jackson County recalled leading religious song services in school buildings when he was a young man around 1910 to 1915:

It fell my place to lead the singing. I got right up there on the floor to lead the singing barefooted and my britches rolled up above the ankles. People never thought no more about that than they would going to the table to eat today.

Times were hard then. The grown girls would walk barefooted to within sight of the schoolhouse and sit down and put their shoes on and come on. When the meeting was over, just as quick as they got out of sight, they'd pull them shoes back off. Times was so hard their daddies and mamas couldn't get them none.

Since shape-note singing was already much in vogue by the 1910s, these singers likely used songbooks published by pioneer advocates of the seven-note system of musical annotation. The availability of these songbooks led to the creation of singing schools, another social and religious institution that was important during the late nineteenth century and the first fifty years of the twentieth century.

Singing schools were typically sponsored by churches in the individual communities. A teacher versed in the rudiments of shape-note music and often representing such music companies as James D. Vaughan and Stamps-Baxter taught adults and children alike the fundamentals of sight reading music and singing the words to the tunes as indicated by the shapes of the notes. Such schools lasted from ten to fourteen nights, serving not only as a religious function but providing much-needed social diversion as well. Many courtships and marriages resulted from fellows walking their favorite girls home after the music and singing lessons at church. Over the past twenty to thirty years these venerated singing schools began to give way to an evening of television at home for adults, cruising in the county seat towns by teenagers, and singings in local schools and churches by gospel trios and quartets.

A typical church singing was held at the Freewill Baptist Church in Hanging Limb, Tennessee, in May 1976. The driveway was filled with cars as residents of this mountain-like community filed into the modest clapboard structure. About eighty persons were present when the singing began. The pastor of the church led the congregational singing from Ruth Shelton's *Best Loved Songs and Hymns*, published in Dayton, Tennessee. He also served as master of ceremonies for the remainder of the evening. Several individuals and singing groups performed during the course of the service, accompanying themselves either with guitar or piano. They sang recent country gospel songs committed to memory or used shape-note hymnals, paying no attention to the notes per se.

More women than men participated in the singing, and several of the groups comprised brothers and sisters. After all singers and musicians present had performed their rehearsed contributions, requests were taken from people in the audience. An open invitation was then given for anyone in the audience to sing or play. A congregational song followed, and a prayer of dismissal was said.

The evening reflected the participants' deep sense of community and healthy outlook on life. Singers and musicians of all ages and ranges of musical ability took part. It was clear that the event was not a platform for performance by the best musicians but a time when individuals could share a common faith and enjoy a period of fellowship—a time for strengthening family and community bonds.

Such times of togetherness, whether at church or in the one-room elementary and small community-based high schools, represented periods of social bonding that were crucial in an era of relative isolation. Though schools and churches continue in the present to serve basic social needs, as a result of cosmopolitan influences they have lost much of the commitment to community found in their earlier counterparts.

CHAPTER

Matters of Life and Death

FOLK MEDICAL PRACTICES

In order to insure health and longevity, early generations in the Upper Cumberland looked to the land to provide medicines and cures for illnesses and bodily injuries. Some of the these remedies were known about and brought to the frontier from the seaboard colonies or the Old World; others were developed as the people became familiar with the area's flora and fauna.

The Upper Cumberland had few medical doctors and nurses until the advent of improved roads beginning with the second and third decades of the twentieth century. Before that, residents had to rely on their own concoctions or trust the practices of "herb doctors," "root doctors," and "bloodstoppers" who claimed to have special skills and certain magico-powers. Actually, such people were seldom referred to by these names; they were simply believed to have healing abilities and were called on in times of need. Their medicinal practices often stemmed from early religious or ritual behavior. Even today's practitioners, along with numerous other residents of the region, feel that "the Divine Creator did not put us here without a remedy for every ailment."

These days, many of the beliefs and sayings related to folk medicine are simply repeated without being wholeheartedly believed, and various practices continue to survive without relevance or meaning. Yet it is impossible to overlook the "natural" and "magical" beliefs that still play an important role in today's holistic medical practices for, despite the modern technology and scientific knowledge that characterize late-twentieth-century medical systems here and elsewhere, the influences of herbalists and shamans who practiced in past years are still evident.

Even when scientific medicine is readily available, people here, as elsewhere around the globe, continue to rely to some extent on traditional healing practices. Given the high costs of modern medicine, economics may be a factor, but confidence in the curing powers of a local folk practitioner or healer must play at least an equal role in an individual's choice to use folk medicine. "Whether it is faith, magic, or superstition," folklorist John Morgan writes, "belief is still the prime ingredient of folk medicine."

Upper Cumberland families of early days collected herbs the year around; however, since many plants were not easily spotted without their summer foliage, most were gathered from late spring to late fall. Geographer Eugene Wilhelm notes that in earlier times only enough plants would be gathered by individual Appalachian families to carry them through the winter. Although all members of the family worked to collect the plants, or their appropriate parts, there was a division of labor involved in the process. The men generally sought out the roots and barks, which were sold to a local storekeeper. Women and children, and sometimes men too, concentrated on gathering plants and herbs to be used by the family.

Home remedies were made from such natural ingredients as the bark from certain trees, especially dogwood, hickory, red oak, sweet gum, wild cherry, and willow; roots of such plants and herbs as blackberry, burdock, ginger, ginseng, Indian clover, Indian turnip, ironweed, jimsonweed, pokeberry, puccoon, raspberry, sarsaparilla, sassafras, snakeroot, spice wood, willow, wahoo, and yellowroot; and herbs including beech drops, cockleburs, cow heel, dandelion, dog fennel, dogwood berries, mullein, pennyroyal, poke berries, ragweed, sedgegrass, and sheepshire [sheep sorrel].

For asthma, people wore an asafetida bag around the neck, drank tea made from rabbit tobacco or life everlasting, or ate a mixture of vinegar, egg white, butter, and honey. They stopped bleeding by filling the cut with soot or spider webs and treated a burn by covering it with soda and molasses, smearing it with cow manure and sweet milk, rubbing on a salve made from cooked dog's hair and lard, or applying a scraped Irish potato. Coughs were treated with a syrup made from pine needles or scaly hickory bark, among many other remedies. For diaper rash it was customary to pulverize the dirt from a dirt dauber's nest and dust the baby's bottom with it or powder the baby with dirt taken from an old mud chimney. Tea made from dog fennel, raspberry leaves, or blackberry roots was a sure cure for diarrhea, and treatments for earache included pouring urine or blowing tobacco smoke into the ear. The inflammation caused by fever blisters typically responded to an application of wax taken from one's ear; parched corn was good for heartburn; applications of poke root juice or sulphur and lard were prescribed treatments for the seven-year itch. Measles responded best to a tea brewed from a red corn cob, sulphur, spicewood, wild sage, or the droppings from sheep (called "sheepnanny tea"), and death from snake bite could be averted if a chicken was cut open and its warm flesh placed on the bite, or the patient was given sweet milk mixed with crushed cocklebur, or the bite was soaked in coal oil until the oil turned green (or the patient got "dead drunk at once" from downing whiskey).

Corn whiskey was a common cure for many ailments, many of which were feigned, people say. A mixture of whiskey and honey was used to treat toothaches, sore throats, and minor stomach ailments. It is reported that Aunt Polly Williams, Gainesboro hotel proprietress, kept a vial of whiskey on her mantel for such purposes. Oral Page of Tompkinsville told of a rural physician before the turn of the century who advised a sick man to "drink pure corn whiskey off bark and roots." The patient went out and got some bark, roots, and herbs and neatly piled them up in a small closet under the stairway. He then placed his gallon jug of whiskey on top of the pile.

Each time the fellow went to the doctor for a checkup, the doctor would ask, "Are you still drinking the whiskey off the roots and bark?"

"Yes sir, yes sir," the fellow responded, "I'm drinking it right off the top of them!"

Well into the twentieth century, residents of the Upper Cumberland possessed a medical vocabulary that would sound strange now, even to most present-day people who grew up there. Most of the folk terms listed in Abraham Verghese's *Folk Medical Lexicon of South Central Appalachia* (1990) were commonly employed in the Upper Cumberland. A sampling of such terms includes blind staggers (dizziness, lightheadedness), brain fever (encephalitis, meningitis), bumfuzzled (confused mental state), catarrh (sinus trouble), change of life (menopause), clap (venereal disease), colic (indigestion, abdominal pain), consumption (tuberculosis), dropsy (heart trouble), fits (seizures), flux (diarrhea), galloping consumption (likely a form of lung cancer), gaulded (heat rash), goozle (Adam's apple), heebie jeebies (nervous condition), knocked up (pregnant), lights (hog lungs), locked bowels (badly constipated), make water (urinate), midlin' (feeling badly; no energy), puny (sick-like; no energy), ptisic (asthma-like conditions), risin' (a boil), running off (diarrhea), scours (diarrhea), St. Vitus dance (jerky movements of arms and legs), stone bruise (sore on bottom of foot), tired blood (fatigue), tolerable (feeling minimally good), trots (diarrhea), work on (castrate).

These and dozens of other ailments or conditions were prevalent throughout the Upper Cumberland. Many folk cures were practical and beneficial; others were based on unsubstantiated custom and practice. Verifiable and nonverifiable medicinal practices alike were used by local herbalists and certain physicians throughout much of the nineteenth century. Unquestionably, many of these medicines served as placebos.

Magico-religious practices were evident in the Upper Cumberland well into the twentieth century, although they were never as commonly used as natural medicines. "Blow doctors" were known for their abilities to cure rashes and the like; "bloodstoppers" claimed to have a special power to stop bleeding in humans, and sometimes in animals as well, which involved the laying on of hands and the invoking of some mysterious biblical passage.

Richard Glass of Red Bank Store, Cumberland County, Kentucky, told of the time when Hugh Logan of that same community stopped a mule's bleeding. First he rubbed the afflicted animal's neck. "Then he held his hand on it, and said this little verse, and that bleeding just gradually begin to clog up and stop. Now I saw that!"

Mrs. Glass then added, "I remember hearing you talk about that. It was a verse in the Bible. You had to get it up by heart, or you couldn't do it."

As a small boy, I tagged along when my father went to John Hume, a bloodstopper who lived in north central Monroe County, to see if he could stop the profuse bleeding in a small mule my father and grandfather had just "worked on." Hume met us in his front yard and inquired intuitively, "What's wrong, Will?"

My father told him what had happened and asked if he could stop the bleeding. Hume responded that he thought he could, then walked alone around behind his house. He reappeared after five minutes or so and instructed us, "Go on back home, fellows; your little mule should be all right."

It was! The bleeding had stopped and the surface blood had already dried up.

Do-it-yourself veterinary medicine was a widespread practice in the Upper Cumberland. Practically every family did whatever was necessary, from birthing calves to castrating young bulls and boar hogs. Licensed veterinarians were unheard of, although jackleg practitioners were within reach of most communities in times of dire need.

One of the major ailments in cattle was a condition universally known as "hollow tail," in which the cow is sickly, weak, won't eat, and has the scours (diarrhea). The source of the problem is said to be a small worm or insect, seldom if ever seen, that is found in the lower portion of the animal's tail and eats the bone marrow there. In 1961, Emit Cain of Kettle, Cumberland County, Kentucky, described the condition and the remedy:

They's a little germ that starts working on that bone. It's some sort of insect that I've always heard. Old people's told me it was a litty bitty worm, but I never saw anything like that. And I've looked for it in a lot of them. This thing works that bone out of the tail, and it's always in the small part of the tail where it works. And when it works through one joint, it goes on to the next joint. . . . I've seen as many as five joints gone in that tail.

The way we do it, we split the tail with a knife and put turpentine and salt and soot in it. And that stops the hollow tail, and the bone comes back. . . . The cow gets bigger all over. I mean her appetite gets better, and she picks right back up.

A lot of these veterinarians that's went to school loses a lot of these cases we're talking about, this hollow tail. They don't realize they's such a thing as hollow tail. This veterinarian we've got up here [at Burkesville] won't agree with it a-tall! But I have went and saved numbers and numbers of people's cattle that had this hollow tail. I'd try other things first, but they wouldn't get better 'til I laid this knife on there and split it, and put the medicine on there. Then they would get better after I done that.

While there were no trained veterinarians in the Upper Cumberland during the early years of the twentieth century, medical doctors were available in surprisingly large numbers. Even though such practitioners often maintained offices in their own homes, their time was largely spent on horseback going from house to house calling on patients. Since they usually carried their few medicines and instruments in their saddlebags, they were typically referred to as "saddlebag doctors." Dr. W. F. Owsley of Burkesville, who began practicing medicine as a saddlebag doctor in 1901—a time when there was not a single mile of paved highway in Cumberland County—recalled how transportation changed during his initial years of service:

I rode horseback; only way you could get around back then. And if you got up in one of those places and it rained, you had to wait 'til the creek run down before you could come back home.

When backwater was up, I've gone part of the way in skiffs. Get out and walk on to the next place. Or they'd meet me with a mule, then they'd take me by skiff on across to the next place. I come to a horse and buggy pretty soon after I started practicing—maybe 1907. I used that until Mr. Ford came out with that jitney.

When asked to identify some of the early doctors in Cumberland County, Owsley surprised me by saying, "Every telephone pole in the county had its own doctor. Up until I started out, 451 doctors had been in Cumberland County. They were registered. There were two or three doctors in every important community at that time. Sometimes, they just registered as a doctor and went to giving medicine. I know one thing, some of them didn't know a thing about medicine!"

A surprising number of individuals across the Upper Cumberland before 1875 did receive some training at medical schools in Louisville

Dr. W. F. Owsley, Burkesville, began practicing medicine in 1901 and was still active in 1978, when he was photographed making a diagnosis by placing a towel over the patient's exposed chest and listening through the cloth. (Photo by Debbie Gibson)

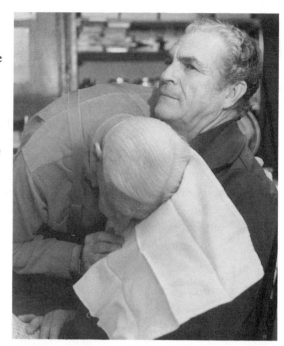

Dr. Owsley demonstrating how he at one time dispensed medicinal powders using a pocket knife (Photo by Debbie Gibson)

and Nashville. Such training was often very brief, however; sometimes no longer than one year. And since there were few restrictions in the registration procedure, practically anyone could claim knowledge of medicine and display an official license.

Three such practitioners in the Free State-Gainesboro area were often featured in an early newspaper column under the names Dr. Pukewell, Dr. Deadner, and Dr. Killumquick. The latter got his name as a result of the time he doctored a young fellow standing on a street in Gainesboro. Upon seeing a festered sore on the lad's foot, the doctor used his pocket knife to lance the afflicted area right there on the street. Bob Dudney of Free State claimed that the patient, who was his brother, almost developed blood poisoning as a result. "From that time on," claimed Dudney, "the doctor was referred to as Killumquick."

None of the three had any medical training. The one called Dr. Pukewell "just picked up an old leather sack and began practicing medicine," Dudney said. "He would use slippery bark elm and pokeberry juice and stuff like that." All three of the doctors at best "just knew how to give people castor oil, quinine, paregoric, baking soda, turpentine, and camphor." These claims are corroborated by Dr. Floyd B. Hay of Albany, who states in *The Country Doctor* that, in his early years of medical practice, those are the sorts of remedies he prescribed.

Before the days of pharmaceutical regulation, then, local doctors prescribed, compounded, and dispensed their own medicines. In 1980, Dr. Oris Aaron of Columbia wrote in *A Patient Booklet* that "the use of herbs, metals, and crude rituals gradually gave way to a new idea of supportive treatment" about 1915. That was the year, according to Aaron, "after which the average patient had a 50-50 chance of being benefitted by an encounter with a physician."

Dr. Owsley recalled that most families were well stocked with their own supply of patent and natural medicines:

Every home had some medicine. People could go into a drugstore and buy most of the common medicines of the day—for earache, diarrhea, boils, aches, bowels, and so on. People were pretty well fixed in a way. They had pert near what we doctors used, and they knew how to use it. They kept quinine right on the table. You could buy that right over the counter. They kept that because the country was full of malaria fever, and quinine was one of the best remedies.

Now, let me tell you something! They've made big progress in surgery, but they haven't added much to medicine.... Seldom you went into a home that didn't have yellowroot for sore mouth. It's one of the best things in the world for sore mouth. They'd take one of those roots and go around chewing it. It's good for an upset stomach.

They also used several other kinds of roots. But for worms, I had a private formula; used saintnide [?] and calomel. I mixed it without even weighing it, and made it into a powder. I said, "Now you give this powder tonight and then follow it up with a dose of castor oil. We never had any trouble. You got the worms, too!

Because hospital facilities in the region were scarce until well into the twentieth century, surgery was often performed in the home. It is said that Dr. Jack Winningham of Russell County performed brain surgery at a patient's home in 1862. Dr. Owsley commented that he personally had conducted numerous operations in patients' homes, ranging from tonsillectomies to the amputation of limbs. In his early years, narrator Bob Dudney underwent a home appendectomy performed by a physician from Nashville.

Another aspect of healing involved mineral waters and the attendant resort facilities. Sick and "puny" members of well-to-do families often went for treatment to these mineral water resorts scattered across the region. Such areas served as fashionable retreats for the socially elite and were often as popular as Hot Springs, Arkansas. The spacious hotels with their uncrowded grounds and porches lined with locally crafted settees and rockers were perfect hideaways for a day, a week, or a month.

Resort centers of some repute in Kentucky were located at Russell Springs in Russell County and at Sulphur Well, Metcalfe County. Those in Tennessee included Bon Air Springs in White County, said to be "the finest resort in the South" at one time; Bloomington Springs, located between Double Springs and Baxter, Putnam County; Hermitage Springs situated in western Clay County; and neighboring Red Boiling Springs, Macon County.

Red Boiling Springs, sometimes referred to as "nature's clinic for sick people," was widely known for the reputed restorative properties of its several varieties of mineral waters. Named for a red bubbling spring, its fame began about 1840 when Shepherd Kirby, a local fellow, supposedly cured an infected eye by bathing in its waters. There are four (or five, depending on whether or not one variety is counted) types of medical waters available in Red Boiling Springs: freestone, red, white, black sulphur, and double-and-twist. The first is entirely free of minerals and is said to be soft with a pleasant taste. Red water was prescribed for diseases of the urinary tract, kidney problems, Bright's disease, diabetes, cystitis, and rheumatism. White water was used to treat dyspepsia, and the black variety was recommended as a cure for gall bladder or stomach trouble and constipation. As for the double-and-twist water, some say that the person who drinks it will grab the stomach and double over, dancing and twisting in agony. Others claim that this water will relieve swelling in afflicted parts of the body, restore sight to the blind, cure pyorrhea of the gums, and eliminate poison from the system, among other miraculous cures.

Businessmen and investors rushed in when Red Boiling Springs's fame began to spread. The town grew from one hotel in 1860 to eight hotels and more than a dozen boardinghouses in its heyday. A boomtown from the Victorian era to the beginning of the Great Depression, this health resort was visited by thousands of people each year. Many still go there, as the mystique lives on. A brochure issued by promoters of the Folk Medicine Festival, organized in 1985 as an annual event, states that "Southern hospitality here means long, white porches overlooking ancient oaks on well-kept lawns; gracious ladies serving icy lemonade, abundant, simple food served from steamy bowls; and most important, 'real people' who are genuinely friendly." To this day, people still visit Red Boiling Springs and the other mineral resorts of the area with gallon jugs and thermos bottles in hand so they can take home the health-giving waters.

In an article in *Tennessee Folklore Society Bulletin*, Richard Raichelson comments on people's belief in and the efficacy of folk medicine. He writes that "belief in the effectivity of home remedies lies not only in the trust placed in a medical tradition but also in the fact that the remedies were seen as actually working whether they were . . . or not. Perhaps faith carries the most weight with regard to belief and effectivity. As a Canadian healer explained, 'What it all boils down to is if you have faith in what you're doing, then you'll get ahead with it.' His comment also seems applicable for the kind of medicine you choose."

Indeed faith is a major component in folk medicine, but is not the same true regarding today's scientific medicine as well? In the past, the scientific medical community looked down on most folk medicine as, at the least, superstition and, at the most, outright quackery. "Only recently, however," writes folklorist John Morgan, "has the modern medical community given serious consideration to the merits of folk medicine. Recent research has shown that folk medicine of world cultures is based on a knowledge more empirical than formerly believed, and that this knowledge is an integral part of the whole cultural system."

WHEN DEATH COMES

All types of medical treatments and practices, all forms of socialization and recreation, and all varieties of religious beliefs and doctrines notwithstanding, death, of course, eventually claims victory. Though few people are ever ready for this event, those with strong religious persuasions appear to approach it with the greatest degree of calmness and assurance.

"The old account was settled long ago" are words from an ageless gospel song that most people of the Upper Cumberland can identify with and lean on as they approach the end. Certain measures are taken during the other life stages in preparation for this last journey. Long before "the crossing" comes, arrangements are made for one's interment or "burial," as it is referred to in the Upper Cumberland. In early years when travel could be a problem during winter months, the site would likely be "over on the hill there with Mommy and Daddy and little Ben," a reference to a small family plot begun when a dying family member had requested burial close to home. This was a common occurrence in a region where ties to the family, the home, and the land remained strong. George A. Knight's *Album of Memories* contains the following account of family burials in the same hallowed plot of ground:

> We were a family that kept up with our ancestors and kept alive their histories. We knew where our ancestors lived and where they were buried.... Grandfather Knight was buried in the Knight Cemetery on the hill above Father's house. This was where Father and Mother wished to be interred and where my baby brother, Lonzo, was tenderly placed. Loved ones that found this to be their final resting place also were Uncle James and Aunt Mattie's little daughter, sister Cora's baby, and aged, fragile Aunt Sarah.

Because heirlooms form such a vital part of family life here, it is common practice for someone to prepare a written list of family artifacts, along with the names of children, and sometimes grandchildren, who are to inherit them. In some instances, especially when furniture is involved, each piece is labelled with the intended recipient's name on it. Such a method of identification is a folk "will," to be considered legally binding and honored by all concerned. Anyone who dares tamper with such an arrangement may risk being shot—literally!

Events surrounding a death take on great social importance in the Upper Cumberland, as the community and the family are drawn especially close during the time of sickness, the event itself, and all the activities associated with the funeral. Rituals and beneficient customs surrounding death and burial are numerous and frequently elaborate. Although their origins are often obscure and puzzling, it is clear that such customs exist to show that the individual, family, and community are inextricably interwoven. Helping others in times of need insures that the same forms of caring and sharing will be extended to oneself when a similar situation arises. Too, helping others during such times of stress is often the result of a system of beliefs and rules of decorum that cannot easily be broken without producing feelings of unease in the offender.

The Upper Cumberland, like other portions of the Upper South, is a rich storehouse of death and burial customs. When a member of the family becomes "deathly ill," or "sick unto death," word is sent to the nearest kin living elsewhere. Once sent telegrams, nowadays these people are called by telephone. It is customary for them to make plans to return home immediately to be with the sick person and to stay until death occurs and the funeral has been conducted.

In earlier times, as death approached, two or three friends or relatives "set up" all night with the sick person, usually in an adjacent room. In some cases, this was done for the benefit of the sick; more typically, however, it was behavior meant simply to bind members of the community together. During these sessions, cards were played and tall tales and off-color jokes were told. Sometimes people still sit up with the very sick, even in hospitals where they may be compelled to confine their visiting to small lounge areas located near the terminally ill friend or relative. Traditions do not die; they are merely altered to conform to contemporary situations.

When death occurs, there are steps that must be taken immediately. For many years, and well into the twentieth century, mirrors in the room were often covered, perhaps to prevent the reflection of the corpse in one of them. Another custom was to stop the hands of the nearest clock at the moment death occurred by obstructing the hands or pendulum with a piece of wood or folded cloth or paper. This was done to prevent the death of another family member within the year. Although it was not spoken of, stopping the hands of the clock probably symbolized the end of time for the family member whose life had been stopped by greater hands. Whatever the explanation, the clock was not started again until the funeral was over. If the deceased had worn dentures, these were found and placed back in the mouth to prevent the jaws from sagging, and a cloth was tied around chin and head to prevent the mouth from coming open. Another procedure that had to be followed almost immediately was the placing of quarters or half dollars on the eyelids of the deceased so as to keep the eyelids closed and, according to some, to insure a peaceful rest for the spirit. These coins were seldom buried with the dead. They were sometimes kept as mementos of the dead person or were later spent as ordinary coins.

By early afternoon or evening the news of a death in the community would have made the rounds, and neighbors would begin arriving, typically with cooked food in hand. Once a decision had been made regarding funeral arrangements, it was customary until the 1930s for a neighbor to go to the church the deceased had attended and toll the bell. The bell was not permitted to ring fully, making its typical "ding, dong" sound. Instead, only the "dong" was sounded, one time for each year of age of the deceased. I can recall as a small boy during the Depression years hearing the bell at Skaggs Creek Church begin to toll and intently listening for the total number of dongs so as to be able to guess the likely identity of the deceased. Preparation would be made immediately by my parents, grandfather, and others in the community to go and assist the family at this time of greatest need.

Many local people knew how to take charge of the body and prepare it for burial, a process known as "laying out the corpse." Depending on the gender of the dead person, two or more women or men of the community bathed the body, fixed the hair, and dressed the body for public viewing and interment. Family members seldom took part in these proceedings. After the bed linens had been changed, the room aired, and other household chores attended to, the body was placed on the bed to await the arrival of the casket, or coffin, as it was often called.

Lena Howell Martin of Gainesboro offered the following description of laying out a corpse:

> When I was a child they'd have two homemade chairs that was strong enough to hold anything. And they [the neighbors] would lay a big board out—a big broad sandboard—when a person would die. And then they'd tie their feet together with a cloth, and tie their hands down. Then they would lay them out on this cooling board for the natural heat to go out [of the body] and be cooled.
>
> They'd have sacks about. And they'd make a little sack about six by eight [inches], put salt in that and lay it on the stomach. And they'd have a bowl or something with soda and water in it, and they'd wet a cloth in that and lay it on their face. When that'd dry out, they'd do it again.

Henry Guffey of Wayne County made caskets during most of his adult life. His 1965 description of some of the older casket forms provides insight into popular tastes of earlier years:

> I have been making coffins for people for about forty years. During all of that time I guess I've made about three hundred coffins. I usually use poplar lumber to make the coffin and box.
>
> The coffin was more or less diamond shaped. I begin by laying off the bottom [foot] part and then shaped the head part. The head and foot were shaped from bottom to top. You cut on the inside to form the sides. The lid part was a raised lid made out of a plank that was shaped from the inside. It came down and fit over the sides with a raised part of about two inches in the center.
>
> The coffin was lined with black satin on the outside, and padded on the inside with cotton. And there was no way to seal these coffins; you just closed the lid. The box was just a square box made from poplar lumber. All of the lumber I used was hand dressed.
>
> When I make coffins, it generally takes me and two helpers about five hours to complete. My original price for a coffin was thirty dollars, but now most of the coffins I make average about one hundred dollars.

Coffins were made from yellow poplar or walnut lumber by one or more persons in the community, often from the supply of lumber stored in their barns for this purpose. Local grocery store proprietors typically stocked the appropriate hardware, such as metal handles and screws for the casket exteriors, and lace, linen, and satin for interior linings. Some stores stocked these items well into the 1970s, for even after factory-built caskets were introduced, they were often brought in with untrimmed interiors.

So that the casketmaker would know what size box to construct, the length and width of the body were measured by a neighbor, who then took the measurements to the carpenter. Often one long stick was used to measure the corpse, being cut off at the appropriate length; then a notch was cut into the stick to indicate shoulder width. What was charged for these early burial containers is not known, but it is generally said that they were donated to the bereaved families by the individual craftsmen. It is recorded that Daniel Clark, a furniture maker and resident of Sparta during the nineteenth century, sold the coffins he made for $2.50 each.

Some individual carpenters personally saw to it that, when they left this world, they would depart in style and comfort, having placed in basements, back rooms, or barn lofts coffins they themselves had built. Made from the finest hardwoods available, these examples of their work showed the strength and pride of their builders. Care was also taken with the linings of the coffins' interiors.

At times, women as well as men preferred to have their caskets constructed in advance of death. Sometimes these burial containers were used to meet more pressing needs. One old fellow from the Ft. Run section of western Monroe County kept his self-made casket in the corner of his living room, hidden from view by a sheet hanging from the ceiling. Tired of waiting to die, he began storing onions in the casket. In a similar vein, a Tennessee woman began using her coffin as a flower bed while she awaited death.

Once a casket was ready, the body was placed in it and set in the living room or front hall of the house with the lid left open so that everyone present could view the corpse and see what objects (jewelry, pictures, toys) had been placed in the casket for interment with the deceased. Many persons who came to pay their respects to the dead and make condolences to the survivors stayed throughout the afternoon and evening until the body had been interred. This custom was usually referred to as "setting up with the dead," and extended through the night so that family members could retire or console each other privately. Many present-day people consider this a somewhat gruesome practice that was best left to primitive ancestors.

Sometimes this vigil was kept with very little talking and moving around. At other times, perhaps depending on the identity of the deceased, the wake (not a common local term) provided a chance to share favorite, often humorous, reminiscences about the one who lay in state.

Although a wake allowed mourners to accept the finitude of life and the reality of death, and perhaps provided an opportunity to pray for the entrance of the deceased into heaven, it may very well be that some early wakes were also held as social events. Many members of the community who were not emotionally involved in the death certainly anticipated the wake as a night of revelry. Some drinking, along with storytelling, games, and amusements served to pass the time until morning and to keep people awake. Merriment and games often mocked death but were not perceived to show disrespect to the dead or the family.

Certain vestiges of these group activities were common through the 1950s, and some are still practiced in county-seat funeral homes. After old friends sign their names in the guest register, they view the deceased, commenting about his or her physical appearance. They then shake hands with or embrace family members present. Male visitors often congregate in the lounge area of the funeral parlor where, over numerous cups of coffee or soft drinks, they continue the common tradition of recounting favorite stories told by or about the deceased. There is no finer tribute to the dead than this contemporary form of the wake, for these storytellers gather out of respect for their departed friend.

By the early 1960s, services conducted in funeral homes had just about eliminated the at-home funerals. The home church of the deceased still functions in this capacity in many instances, however, as most funeral home directors remain willing to transport the body to a church for the final ceremony if the family prefers it.

A police car leads the way to the church or cemetery in urban areas, followed by the hearse and private automobiles in descending order of kinship to the deceased, all headlights on. The same order is followed in rural areas, except that police escorts are fairly rare. Whether urban or rural, it is usual throughout the Upper Cumberland for drivers of all types of vehicles meeting the funeral procession to come to a complete stop and wait until all cars with headlights on have passed by. This custom, not required by law, is thought by some to be based on superstition and fear of the unknown.

I shall not soon forget being a part of the funeral cortege of my beloved friend and research helper, Ona Barton, of Forbus, Tennessee, in 1991. Once the memorial services for Ona had been concluded at a funeral home in Jamestown, two dozen cars lined up behind the hearse to make the sixteen-mile trip to the cemetery at Forbus. As the drivers carefully navigated the treacherous curves going down Jamestown Mountain, we were met by an eighteen-wheel logging truck loaded down with cargo. The steep hill notwithstanding, the respectful trucker brought his

heavily loaded vehicle to a complete standstill as the funeral procession moved down the mountainside. Then, just before we reached the cemetery where Ona would be laid to rest beside her husband, a farmer plowing a field adjacent to the highway stopped his tractor until the mourners had all passed by.

A Clinton County funeral procession (Photo by Larry Powell)

Drivers who are following the funeral procession but are not a part of it are expected to remain behind until the cortege reaches its final destination. In the event of lengthy trips to the cemetery, cars in the funeral party often are spaced so as to allow other drivers to pass should they desire to do so.

In earlier times, it was believed that stopping the funeral procession for any reason signified that death would come to another in the funeral party within a year. It was also thought that people would have bad luck if they viewed a cortege through a window, pointed their finger at one, allowed their shadow to fall on the hearse, or watched it until it was out of sight. If any of these violations occurred, bad luck could be averted if one crossed one's fingers and spit, touched a button, turned around and walked backwards, or whispered a prayer.

"Such beliefs have largely disappeared today," writes folklorist Janice Molloy, "but it is still customary to stop for a funeral." This custom, based on ancient folk belief and practice, is presently a "special way in which we show respect for the dead."

Whether the final service is conducted at the funeral home or in a church, there is music by a group of invited singers, eulogizing by a minister, and then more singing while those in attendance pass slowly by the casket to view, weep openly, and pay their last respects to the deceased. When all the onlookers have gone by, family members move in closely to take a final look at the departed relative and perhaps leave a kiss or caress before the funeral director closes the casket lid.

Chairs are generally provided at the graveside for the bereaved family members; others stand, encircling the open grave. A passage from the Bible is read aloud, a brief devotional is given by the minister, and then the casket is slowly lowered on ropes into the grave. This part of the burial ritual has remained essentially unchanged throughout the history of the Upper Cumberland. At one time, it was customary for a close relative, generally the surviving spouse or child, to toss or shovel the first bit of earth onto the top of the casket. In some instances, family members were then led away from the scene as the gravediggers and other members of the community went to work to fill the open grave with the fresh red dirt. Traditionally, however, relatives remained at the site all the while so as to be the first to place a floral tribute (if fresh flowers were in season) on the newly mounded grave.

The burial completed, relatives and friends usually went home with the family. Almost always, there was adequate food, as many dishes of meat and vegetables had been brought in throughout the period. Many of these visitors stayed on for days or even weeks to help ease the family's burdens and to provide them with emotional support during this stressful time. By and large, however, the demands of small town and farm life and labors insured a rapid return to normalcy.

Now unused although still maintained by caring descendants, the family graveyards mentioned earlier eventually gave way to community cemeteries across the region. In recent years, however, memorial gardens have appeared and, because their ground-level grave markers make groundskeeping and maintenance far easier, they may in the near future replace the community burial plots. It is in the two earlier cemetery types, however, that folk ideas are more commonly embodied.

Standard early practices employed in both the family and community burial plots included the marking of graves with unlettered, whitewashed fieldstones; the mounting of photographs of the deceased on the fronts of gravestones (1880s to 1940s); the fencing off of designated family burial plots with hand-chiseled rectangular stones removed from limestone or sandstone quarries; and the covering of graves with small wooden buildings or stone structures that give the appearance of buildings.

These tiny, wooden gabled buildings, typically called gravehouses, were erected over a single in-ground burial (grave) or over as many as six of the members of one family. Three cultural sources—European, African, and American Indian—may have influenced the use and distribution of these gravehouses, which began to appear around 1840. Like many of the older folk architectural forms used by previous generations in the Upper Cumberland, these relics are rarely seen today.

Stone grave coverings include the rectangular "box grave," resembling an above-ground vault. Grave houses of this variety are often termed "peaked graves," "slab graves," "sandstone graves," "cattle rocks," "hog troughs," and "comb graves." Although they are sparsely located in certain parts of Alabama, Arkansas, and Texas, these traditional prismatic grave structures more than any other single cultural feature lend uniqueness to the folk cemeteries in the Upper Cumberland.

Box graves are constructed of sandstone slabs held together with iron rods or built entirely of quarried sandstone or limestone blocks. Once the walls are completed, one large rock or concrete slab is placed on top, thus covering the entire grave. These structures have been spotted across the region, but Overton County appears to be their center of distribution.

Coffin-shaped grave structures similar to box graves can also be found in the region, however rarely. Some are made of a single, solid rock, hewn to resemble a six-sided coffin; examples can be seen in the Gamaliel Cemetery in southern Monroe County. Other coffin-shaped grave coverings include those built with numerous hewn stone blocks and those constructed from single rock slabs large enough to form one entire side of the structure. All examples of this second coffin-shaped variety are capped with a single, six-sided rock slab.

A very rare variety of stone grave covering was constructed with handhewn limestone to form a house-like edifice atop the grave. While they may have been used elsewhere in the region, I have spotted them only in southern Cumberland County, Kentucky. Dates of their origins and their subsequent uses are unknown; names and dates of the deceased are typically missing.

In some early world cultures, people may have built gravehouses to control the spirits of the deceased. However, the function of these local ones appears to have been to keep pigs, dogs, and other scavenging animals, as well as medical school students in need of cadavers, away from the corpse. In at least one instance, the parents of a teenage boy

Cemetery landscape in southeastern Overton County

A gravehouse over a family plot in Overton County

Prismatic grave covers, southern White County, 1991.

Mausoleum-like grave sheds, southeastern Overton County

All photos on pages 118-19 by the author

who accidentally shot himself in Pickett County erected a gravehouse to prevent water from reaching his body.

Before World War II, families continued to honor their dead by annually cleaning the graves, mounding up or leveling them with fresh dirt, and decorating them with jars or tin cans filled with wild or domesticated flowers. In the absence of these, most families made artificial flowers from brilliantly colored crepe paper. These were dipped in paraffin for protection from the sun and unfavorable weather for a few weeks. After the war, when times and living conditions in the Upper Cumberland underwent drastic changes, plastic funeral flowers were introduced. Nowadays virtually every gravestone is adorned with one or more of these plastic arrangements, so that each cemetery comes alive with radiant color on or just before Decoration Day, or the Thirtieth of May as some older residents call it. Perhaps unaware that these arrangements are often secured on the gravestones with metal frames that rust and stain the stones, many individuals within the community seem to compete with friends and neighbors for most elaborate decorations on their family burial plots.

One other folk custom associated with mourning is the practice of writing bereavement verse one or more years after the death of a beloved family member and paying by the word to have the commemorative verse printed in the want-ads section of a local newspaper. Here are two such verses taken from *The Tompkinsville News* in the late 1980s:

IN MEMORY OF ALTIE ARTERBURN

Gone, but never to be forgotten
While life and memory last,
Is our kind and loving mother
And the happy days long past.
Ottie, Ezma, Fred and Dean

IN MEMORY OF LILLIE T. BURKS

A precious one from us is gone,
A voice we loved is stilled;
A vacant place is in our hearts,
Which never can be filled.
Sadly missed by her family: Son and Daughter,
Dorcie and Dewayne and her grandchildren

Another way to assuage grief is to have published a narrative statement about a person's death in a form somewhat similar to the obituary announcements commonly found in daily and weekly newspapers. Narrative statements are different from obituaries in that they are written by someone, usually a relative, who is unashamedly grieved and who wants the community to share in these feelings of despair. While not nearly as popular as bereavement verse, at least not in recent years, the narrative announcements serve the same function; they help to allay grief by providing a confrontation with the issue of separation by death. Some of these written tributes are brief; others are lengthy. The following appeared in a 1936 issue of the *Jackson County Sentinel* under the heading "Our Baby":

On Tuesday, January 20 at 5:30 p.m. death claimed my precious little baby from our home. We had only been in from the West a month when she died, leaving me and a little sister three years old. I am so sad and lonely without her. She was only fifteen months old. Her death came after a few days illness with spinal trouble and congestion of the brain. The funeral was held at my home and the little remains were laid to rest in the George Graveyard. I hope to meet little baby in Heaven someday, where there will be no more sorrow, parting or pain.

Her Mother, Lyra Young

Another narrative announcement included in that newspaper the same year was captioned, "Her Mama's Photograph." The first line reads like the introduction to a broadside ballad or a sentimental song: "Please, can't I have mama's photograph first, before they put me to sleep."

After reading a verse penned in memory of his sister by Quinn Davidson of Chanute, Pickett County, I asked where he got the inspiration to write it. "Well, the words will just come to you," he commented, "and you commence to kinda blocking it out. Very often I'll rub out a word and add another one in." I also talked with certain persons who admitted to borrowing words, ideas, actual phrases, and metaphors from previously published verses.

In spite of all the tears shed and the long days and nights often spent alone by survivors, people of the Upper Cumberland seek and find sustenance in their treasured memories of the deceased family member. Stories about the dead become such a vital component of the survivors' memories that family legend cycles are often built around the personalities and character traits of the deceased. The dead are often portrayed in bigger-than-life terms and seem to be still very much a part of the living scene. Through the early years of the twentieth century, group photographs of family members would often feature someone, typically the surviving spouse, prominently displaying a framed picture of the deceased.

Many of the older traditional medicinal practices, along with the beliefs and customs associated with death and burial, such as preparing the corpse, sitting up with the dead, and hauling the corpse to the grave, have been displaced in recent years by scientifically trained medical doctors and professional funeral directors. The result of those social interactions—the unifying group activities—was a closeness among family and community members that has slipped away in the face of a more accelerated way of life during the latter half of the twentieth century.

Times Just Aren't the Way They Used to Be

In 1961, Darlene Botts Carter, a resident of north central Monroe County, spoke the words that make up the title of this section. We were discussing the tradition of narrating tales about the supernatural that once dominated family storytelling events on long winter evenings. If she were alive today, Carter would be even more struck by the changes that have brought the Upper Cumberland closer to mainstream American life and thought.

World War II marked the end of the old way of life in the Upper Cumberland. Numerous male and female veterans never returned to the family farm, choosing instead to cast their lots in the larger cities of the South and Midwest, as did many other residents of the region. Those who remained behind witnessed dramatic alterations in folklife patterns, due largely to the improvement of agricultural technology, the entrance of women into the workplace, changes in musical tastes and other aspects of teen-age entertainment, the disappearance of community schools in the wake of consolidation efforts, and more female influence in family, religious, and social matters.

In the midst of all this change, tradition is alive and well. Folklore operates to insure conformity, even when some of the rules are new, as we will see in the next two chapters.

CHAPTER 6

Folklife of Contemporary Youth

Until the end of World War II, an eighth-grade diploma marked the completion of a successful period of schooling. I still recall the envy I felt as a freshman at Gamaliel High School in 1944 when a former eighth-grade classmate told me that he was earning the fabulous wage of $1.25 an hour at a factory job in Indianapōlis. By then, however, pursuing a high school education was the norm for many young men and women. College attendance, on the other hand, did not become common until the late 1950s.

Urban youngsters who went to high school before the 1940s, and even through the war years, socialized in local restaurants or in a hotel lobby where they played juke boxes and danced or chatted for a couple of hours each afternoon. Country kids often joined them on Saturdays and Sunday afternoons. Katherine Anderson of Gainesboro recalls that during the late 1930s she and her friends hung out at the Hickory Tavern Restaurant and danced the jitterbug, especially when the jukebox played "The Dipsy Doodle." Only pop music was available then. Country music came alive for high school students in the mid- to late 1940s when recording artists such as Eddy Arnold, Kitty Wells, and Hank Williams hit the jukeboxes.

Virtually all high school students during the 1940s and 1950s played together and socialized in nonstratified groups. The only verbalized distinction among secondary school students then was that of "town kids" and "country kids," a dichotomy that had little or no real meaning when it came to socializing and dating. When I was a senior at Tompkinsville High School, a female student told me that her home economics teacher advised the girls in her classes not to date "those country boys." It was common, though, for "town girls" to prefer "country boys," or so we fellows thought.

By the early 1960s the "city high schools" in each of the county seats and the one or two other secondary institutions located across each county had disappeared, the result of a second wave of consolidation. County high schools such as Fentress County High School, Macon

County High School, Monroe County High School, and Wayne County High School came into existence. With the formation of these large educational institutions, along with the introduction of middle schools and predawn bus schedules, it was soon common practice among students to form groups according to affluence, personal tastes, and social practices, a situation that continues into the present.

In conversations with students from nineteen high schools across the Upper Cumberland in 1991, at least five folk groupings were identified at one or all schools. These social categories, each looked on with derision and often disgust by the others, are preps or preppies; jocks; cowboys, country hicks, or just country; hoods or rednecks; and freaks, scums, or scum buckets. Four other categories sometimes included as separate from the above are thrashers or skateboarders; buttheads (cigarette smokers sometimes referred to as scums); burnouts ("burned out on drugs, spaced out, out of touch with reality"); and ag boys ("the ones who hang out around the ag shop all day and talk about cows and farming and things").

While not all schools have the five basic groups, they apparently do have the prep, hick, and scum categories. All students in any one school do not necessarily agree on the same social divisions or the terms used to identify each of them.

Preps are "the people with a lot of money." They are "party animals" (a term sometimes used in place of "preps") who "scope the guys," "wear only the finest clothes and have to have the best of everything." Some see preps as "very conservative in dress"; others describe them as wearing "polo shirts or shirts and pants that don't match." They are known for their preference for rock and rap music but "never agree to being a member of a rock band." Preppies are also known for their good grades; thus some males in this category may be referred to as "geeks."

"Geeks are people that others make fun of," according to an unidentified Macon County High School female.

Michelle Brown, a mid-1980s Macon County graduate, proceeded to explain that "a geek is somebody who wears glasses way down here [on the nose]. Some of them, even, just get glasses because they want them. Geeks are skags—skaggy little people—because they don't know how to dress. Yet, they have clothes that are more expensive than ours."

"They're not real preps," contributed a male standing nearby.

"It's the way they wear their clothes," Michelle continued. "They're forever reaching down here [pointing to the belt line] and tugging on their pants to keep them up high. . . . They wear checkered pants, and their shirts have butterfly collars. You know, them big collars that come way out like this [toward the shoulders]."

The fellow again intruded into the conversation. "A typical geek has got a shirt that's buttoned all the way to the top. He wears a sort of string tie, and he's got an ink pen stuck here in his shirt pocket."

"What's a geek female like?" I asked.

Michelle responded with a hearty chuckle, "A geek girl is a dork, a dorky-like person."

Interrupted at this point by other students who came rushing up to be a part of the scene, I was unable to continue the conversation and obtain further definitions and descriptions. Later that evening, however, another person defined a dork as "a person who dresses weird, bugs you, and stays up all night studying."

If we can assume a degree of commonality across the Upper Cumberland, a dork may also be classified as a "nerd." The latter was described by students in Cumberland and Wayne counties, Kentucky, as a very intelligent person who wears eyeglasses. Nerds "lack common sense because they are unable to deal with other people."

While not all area high schools have the category "rednecks," most schools do, especially those located in the larger towns. "Rednecks are the heaviest drinkers in school," claimed Livingston Academy students Mairlyn Breeding and Martin Evans. They went on to explain that the biggest problems in their high school were drinking and, to a lesser extent, marijuana smoking. Breeding and Evans asserted that rednecks are not very good students and are proponents of rock music.

Redneck affiliation with rock music was also pointed out by Scotty Garrett and Shane Roberts of Cookeville, who characterized rednecks as "nothing but troublemakers who fight all the time." Similar attributes were accorded rednecks by students from Burkesville, Edmonton, and Monticello. There, rednecks are known as "troublemakers, nonconformists, gossipers and rumormongers," according to a Metcalfe County male. Rednecks prefer either heavy metal or contemporary country music, refuse to study, drink a lot, are bigoted and have attitude problems. The term "hoods" is often used to identify such students.

In Clay, Fentress, Jackson, Macon, Monroe, Pickett, Russell, and Smith counties, and perhaps others, the folk label "redneck" is seldom used. Someone suggested that students in these more rural counties recognized that much of their own behavior reflects certain redneck character traits. A group of students from Macon and Smith counties see rednecks as being "just plain old country boys who wear cowboy hats and listen to country music." The term "cowboy" is thus "what rednecks [both male and female] call themselves." The same is true of those students of both genders who are called hicks, country hicks, and sometimes ag boys. They prefer their self-proclaimed labels to the more offensive "redneck." Likewise, "country" is a term seldom used by teens in the Upper Cumberland to refer to self, friend or foe. One person

"Cowboys" hanging out along the cruising strip in Lafayette (Photo by the author)

explained that the reluctance to label anyone country was because almost everyone in the Upper Cumberland region *is* country or has close family ties to the land.

Students in the category variously referred to as freaks, scums, scum buckets, and skanks (members of this group also use the word "freak" in referring to themselves) are always seen as troublemakers, but they are not synonymous in the popular mind with the less-offensive rednecks. It is generally charged that freaks consume a lot of alcohol and use heavy drugs.

"Some of the freaks are *mean*," commented a female cowboy.

"I mean *mean mean*," a second young woman chimed in.

Still a third one charged, "They start fights every day; slash tires and everything."

"Have you talked with any of the freaks?" the first person asked me. [Heavy laughter by the others present.] "You should never talk with the freaks," she admonished me. "They are lowlife, nothing but bitches and 'hos [whores]."

Ironically, while I was talking to and photographing a group of freaks hanging out in front of a street-facing commercial building, one of the males said of the preps and cowboys across the strip, "Those geek women over there are nothing but a bunch of bitches and 'hos." Although the geeks are frequently accused of heavy alcohol consumption, only one of those I chatted with was drinking beer at the time. Others were smoking cigarettes. One fellow observed that he neither smoked nor drank alcoholic beverages, and that he was a freak only because he did not "want to socialize" with the geeks. A female freak confided that she did not have anything to do with the geeks mainly because her brother was one.

Students at Livingston High School do not use the term "geek." Instead, they prefer the term "scum," describing such students as being "uncouth—way out." "Geeks are wild with the wrong people," said a female senior at Livingston. "It's okay to be wild if it's with the right people," she went on. "Just don't be wild with sleazy people." Clearly, a social dichotomy exists across the region between the freaks and all the other groups, especially when they are away from the high school campus.

Certain students at Metcalfe County High School fall into a category referred to as "skanks," a freak-like group that is looked upon with disfavor by most of the student body. Selena and Ginger Nunn, sisters from Edmonton, provided the following list of skank characteristics:

1. They are males who wear earrings.
2. Their hair, usually long, is dyed in two different colors and dressed with gel and other oils.
3. They wear short, black leather jackets, boots outside their jeans, and chains on their boots.
4. Their shirts have holes in them and look dirty.
5. They smell bad, talk dirty, and look as if they're high all the time.
6. They are usually smart but don't try to do their homework. They get thrown out of class a lot.
7. They are identified with devil-worshipping signs.
8. They are into heavy metal music.
9. They have their own walk, and even though they look weird they have girl friends.

Most of today's high school students, like their parents before them, have certain terms they use in describing the physical attractiveness and biological attributes of others, especially those of the opposite gender. Although the terms "foxy" and "sexy" generally disappeared in the 1970s, some of the more rural male students still use them to describe a super good-looking female. "Chick" is still popular for the same purpose, as are "buba," "hot mama," and "bitch" ("Did you see that good-looking bitch in that red car?"). According to two black males in Sparta, "She hittin'" or "She bad" are two ways of describing "a great-looking female."

"Hunk," "sexy," or "gorgeous" remain terms for referring to a good-looking fellow. "Hamburger" describes either male or female "with nice buns," but it is acceptable for students to use more straightforward words, such as "look at that butt," and "look at those tits."

An extremely ugly fellow is referred to as sleazy, sick, gross, gaggy, pukey, or as a scum, dork, geek, jerk, or dog, depending on the school. Ugly women receive some of these same disparaging folk labels, to which may be added "butt-ugly." The term "fugly" is used to describe a fat, ugly person of either sex by some Metcalfe countians and their Green County neighbors to the north.

These diverse social groupings and the terminologies used to distinguish them grew up largely in the 1960's as a result of school consolidation. It is likely, however, that area high schoolers are introduced to the concept of social and economic classes and related in-group behavior during their preteen years. Slumber parties for young girls are the rage by the time they are eight or nine years old. Similar events involving the fellows are typically called "sleepovers." These boys also get together and camp out. Depending on the boys' ages, campouts are held in backyards or in more remote places such as a nearby lakeshore.

Parents and grandparents before them had engaged in similar bonding practices. The slumber party then and now is a composite folk event involving practically all the folklore genres associated with childhood and adolescence. "Staying up late, delving into occult practices, playing pranks—all elements of the slumber party, can be traced back many years and even centuries," writes Julia W. Oxrieder. "But as the sum of its parts, the slumber party as we know it today is a product of the twentieth century."

In February 1992, twenty sixth-grade students at Clinton County Elementary School, Albany, wrote essays describing slumber parties and sleepovers. Stephanie Claborn provided the following account:

> The best slumber party I ever went to was at my cousin's. First of all, we played basketball and baseball. Later we played volleyball, and when I served the ball I hit my cousin in the head. We also told jokes about a farmer and his dog. We told a scary story about this boy and girl who got killed.
>
> We ate pizza and drank cokes, then did a funny dance. I forgot what it was. After that we played on the Ouija board and asked it if somebody was going to go with somebody. We played Spin the Bottle, and my cousin had to kiss this boy she really liked. Finally we called this woman and asked if she knew who we were.
>
> We stayed up until 2:00 or 3:00 in the morning. Then, when I thought we were all asleep, my cousin threw water all over us!
>
> The next morning everyone had to go home. Slumber parties can really be fun.

Misty Winningham's description of a slumber party on her twelfth birthday reveals that the sequence of events, while generally harmless, can get somewhat risqué:

My twelfth birthday party was the best party ever because we did lots of fun things. It was very hot that day. There were about 24 people present at my house for the party. A bunch of them rode the bus home with me. Later that afternoon, other people came.

First, we jumped on the trampoline for about an hour. Then at about 4:30 p.m. all the people were there, so we ate cake and ice cream and drank Mountain Dew. We ate on the trampoline. After that, some people played basketball, while others snuck behind the house and played Truth or Dare. I dared Adam M. and Adam Y. to take off all their clothes and run up and down the road naked. We went to the road and about the time Adam M. had his pants unbuttoned, my mom came out the door.

I said, "Mom, get back in that house right now!"

Right then my mom came out, and Adam Y. ran just as hard as he could to the barn. He got up in the barn loft and wouldn't come down. About a minute later Vicky went up in the loft and got Adam down.

About 7:00 p.m. everyone went home, but Sarah and Vicky stayed all night with me. We called up boys and acted like different people and told them that we liked them. That night about 9:00 we were in bed eating popcorn and we got it all in the bed. The next morning we went to school, and we were so sleepy we acted like we were half dead.

Of the twenty essays, fourteen show food and drink consumption to be a principal bonding activity for the youngsters present. Games, both traditional and new, are described in virtually all the essays, and television viewing is frequently mentioned. Fifth-grader Jeremy Tallent writes, "My Mom put my TV in the den with my Nintendo so I could watch TV and play Nintendo at the same time. . . . My friend John Halcomb and I had the house to ourselves after Mom and Dad went to bed. We started playing Super Mario World at 6 p.m. and played until 2 a.m. Then we watched TV and read books. Mom and Dad were not nearly as excited at 2 a.m. as we were."

Various forms of competitive sports are mentioned in the students' papers; seven referred to jumping on the trampoline, a luxury that has only recently become available to children and teenagers. Dancing, once frowned upon in the region, is alluded to in more than one-half the essays.

For whatever reasons members of the young generation come together, they frequently talk about members of the opposite gender, prank each other on the spot, engage in storytelling sessions that feature jokes and supernatural narratives, and make nuisance telephone calls to friends and adults.

All in all, today's youth engage in the same kinds of folklore practices that their parents and grandparents did, with the expected adaptations and innovations made possible by modern technology and increased parental buying power. Donna Goff of Red Boiling Springs described what took place at typical slumber parties when she was in elementary school beginning in the late 1950s and extending through the mid-1960s:

We would invite a bunch of girls from the schoolhouse, and we just laid around in pajammies and pigged out on a whole bunch of food; stay up all night. Whoever went to sleep first, we would throw ice on their back or something like that.

But during the course of the night we'd play music and dance; fix everybody's hair and makeup; talk about boys we liked; tell jokes, not dirty jokes or racist jokes, just funny ones. Then one time, Mama got us a Ouija board. We'd put our hands on that little thing and ask all these questions.

We did this all through grade school, but had just about stopped by the time we got to high school.

The twenty essays written by the Clinton County elementary students provide good descriptions of the group activities of typical adolescents in the Upper Cumberland region as they continue to develop the social skills that will serve them well in their adult years ahead. The folkways involved with slumber parties/sleepovers serve as developmental tasks of life, in that they constitute healthy and satisfactory growth toward maturity. Having mastered most of the problems of childhood within the slumber party framework, these young people gain confidence in their ability to direct their own lives, and in doing so discover who they are and what they are becoming.

By the time contemporary adolescents reach the ages of thirteen to fourteen, most of them have begun the custom of "hanging out" by the swimming pool during the summer months and at a local shopping mall during colder weather. Youngsters this age sometimes ride around in automobiles driven by older teenagers, an activity referred to as "cruising" both here and in other parts of the country. "It is almost like a rite of passage when you are taken for your first ride down the by-pass in the company of fellow teenagers," writes Sandra Wolford, "rather than seated in the back seat of Mom and Dad's family automobile."

This weekend ritual—driving around a circuit or up and down a strip, parking in an area designated for teen socializing, or simply driving aimlessly—is a relatively young tradition that has developed as motor vehicles have become ubiquitous. At the beginning of the 1990s, this widespread, primarily teenage activity encompasses a wealth of cultural

meaning for folklorists, social historians, and sociologists. One trip to cruising centers such as Lafayette, McMinnville, Russell Springs, and Somerset would provide a researcher with quantities of notes on ritual behavior, oral narratives and testimonials, information on the newest fads in cars and trucks, and an informed vocabulary of sexual nuances.

Although cruising as it is known today came to the Upper Cumberland largely in the mid- to late 1960s, its roots are planted firmly in the 1920s—a period when the automobile changed from being a rich boy's plaything to a middle-class necessity. As folklorist Joe Ruff has noted; evidence that southern country folk in those days were also fascinated by the automobile comes from Grand Ole Opry star Sam McGee, who in 1928 sang "Chevrolet Car":

> When your hair turns gray and your head grows bald,
> You will see that the Chevrolet can beat them all;
> I love you baby, but crazy 'bout my Chevrolet.

Taking a break from cruising in Russell Springs (Photo by the author)

Those who were high schoolers in the mid- to late 1940s and early 1950s, and whose parents could afford an automobile, will recall that weekend courting meant riding up and down the main street a few times, parking around the courthouse square, and stealing a few kisses from the sweet thing nestled alongside. Hank Williams, Sr., sang a cruising song back then called "Settin' the Woods On Fire." A couple of lines ran:

> "We'll sit close to one another,
> Up one street and down the other."

As the automobile became more and more a family institution in the Upper Cumberland, changes in the social order followed. Spontaneous recreation came into vogue and could now accommodate larger groups; family life grew more complicated and more fragmented; and, above all, the mechanics of courtship changed. Riding in the automobile tended to replace the older, more traditional customs of sitting in the parlor in the winter or on the front porch swing during the summer.

Not only was the family car a courtship vehicle, it soon began to serve as a means of satisfying teenagers' restlessness. It was not uncommon, especially for those whose parents condoned such behavior, for a young person to leave home early in the evening and go pick up a buddy, drive around for a few minutes, and then park in front of a jukejoint and go inside to socialize with others there.

Although this is an early form of cruising and hanging out, the term "cruising" apparently was not used before the 1960s. Pat Ganahl, former editor of *Hot Rod* magazine, offered the following commentary:

> Cruising began in rural areas when young men from farms drove into town for the evening. . . . There usually wasn't much happening in these towns, so they'd just drive around in their cars. Because the towns had only one main drag, they'd end up driving down one end and back the other. Pretty soon the girls on the farm started borrowing daddy's car and heading for the main drag too.

It is not known how or when cruising first came to the Upper Cumberland, but it continues to be a favorite pastime. It is a form of play activity that sometimes includes deviant behavior; it contains an aspect of self-testing among the participants; and, thanks to group sanction, it provides for the violation of norms of responsible adult behavior by those who choose to do so. On the other hand, cruising is an activity that is seemingly "age-appropriate and normative" says folklorist Richard Reuss, "though aggravating to parents, police, pedestrians, and polite society."

As a scholar investigating this social phenomenon, I tend to see cruising from the viewpoints of its participants across the Upper Cumberland. I must confess that I was a bit aggravated, however, when I was once stranded in a shopping center's parking lot at Russell Springs, enclosed by a circle of slow-moving cars that were being driven literally bumper to bumper. (It is said that in the early days of cruising, traffic could be stalled for such lengthy periods of time that fights among the cruising set could start and finish before traffic got moving again.) I sat there in my automobile for twenty minutes or so with motor running and lights on, hoping that someone would stop to let me through the circle of cars. Finally, one of the fellows whom I had photographed and talked with earlier that evening saw my plight, came to me, and said, "I'll get you out."

He walked over to the chain of half-moving, half-stalled cars and motioned with his hand for one to stop. It did! He then waved me through and smiled as I saluted gratefully and said, "See you later." Here was a clear demonstration of the camaraderie and mutual respect known and practiced by the cruising set.

Interestingly enough, "cruising" is not the "in" term used to describe this pervasive weekend youth activity. Rather than say to a friend, "Let's go cruising," many of the students, including those who live in town, say simply, "Let's go to town." Translated, this means, "Let's go to the strip and ride around," or "Let's go ride the strip." The terms "town" and "strip" are thus synonymous. Teenagers from Russell County's Lower End section have two uses of the word "town." For them, "going to town" means simply going to a store in Jamestown, the county seat. "Going up town" connotes going to Russell Springs, one of the favorite cruising spots in Kentucky's Upper Cumberland.

Russell Springs is especially important for teens from Liberty, Columbia, and Jamestown, all in Kentucky. When they prefer to cruise in Russell Springs, they'll say, "Let's go to the Springs." Members of these same social sets often go cruising in Campbellsville and/or Somerset, however, because of the availability of beer there.

High schoolers in Cookeville typically say, "Let's go to the mall," said Scotty Garrett. He then added, "Mostly, they just wind up riding up and down the strip." Two black male students in Sparta said that the common calls to weekend activity there are, "Let's ride," and "Let's blaze."

It may be that the term "cruising" was in vogue in certain portions of the Upper Cumberland during the late years of the 1960s and into the 1970s. Jim Bowman of Livingston claimed that the high school generation to which he belonged during those years used the term. "Actually, we just mainly sat on the hoods of our parked cars," he said. "Most people couldn't buy the gas necessary to keep their cars on the move."

Today's teen set typically uses the expressions "hanging out," "settin'," "standing around," and "chillin'" to describe what they are doing when not in moving cars or trucks. One of the black males in Sparta defined "chillin'" as "lettin' it all hang out." This activity involves the carryings-on of a specific small group whose members "are not looking for women or trouble," according to a fellow from Russell County's Lower End. He went on to explain what "cruising" implies. "That's when it's a whole bunch of people [in contrast with hanging out] looking for someone to talk to, or looking for women or men, or looking for a fight. Now that's the way it is!"

Thus cruising actually involves vehicles moving up and down the street and stereo tape players or radios blaring loud rock, rap, or country music that can be heard across town. Added to the din are the sounds of tires squealing on takeoff; motors being revved at high speeds, sometimes without mufflers; squealing brakes and skidding stops on graveled road shoulders; horns blowing; and loud yelling at friends seated in other vehicles or standing alongside the curb. Stops last only long enough for people to shout at each other through rolled-down windows.

Many of the teenagers drink alcoholic beverages, especially as the evening's activities begin to slow down. Although some get drunk, most do not drink to excess. It was said that marijuana and cocaine are used by a few, but I saw no evidence of this at any of the cruising centers documented.

During the course of the evening, those who are hanging out participate in such activities as gossiping, sex boasting when members of the opposite gender are not present, telling dirty jokes, arm wrestling, doing push-ups in the middle of the street, and dancing to music on the car radio.

Approximately one-fifth of these teenagers cruise the strip alone, but the majority of them make the circuits in pairs looking for members of the opposite sex who might be willing to join them for the rest of the evening. One fellow in Lafayette referred to himself and his male companion as "hustlers."

When I asked him to clarify the term, a female standing nearby answered for him, "Try to pick up women; to get women!"

I was informed by numerous cruisers and hangers-out present that evening that picking up members of the opposite sex takes place all the time. At least a half-dozen females told me that they go cruising "to get picked up by a good-looking guy."

Sex sometimes takes place as the culminating event of the evening. Certain spots "out of town," or "down in the [city] holler," to quote two Lafayette cruisers, are frequented for the purpose.

I asked a mixed-gender group of eleven students, who were leaning against parked cars, to identify the worst aspect of cruising and hanging out. They all said that it was the rather vicious gossip at school for the next few days that they dreaded most. They claimed that some students make too much out of what they see or fabricate information to make good gossip.

Cruising normally takes place for approximately five years in each participant's life. It generally begins in earnest when the young person turns fifteen or sixteen, becoming a rite of passage that marks transition to a more advanced life stage. For most, cruising as a folk event ends with high school graduation, though there may be one additional year before it is given up entirely.

Given the lack of recreational resources available for most young married couples in the county seat towns of the Upper Cumberland, it is not surprising that some continue to "go to town" on Saturday nights. Two couples, each with two attendant children, were part of the Lafayette cruising scene during my visits there. And in Russell Springs, I talked with and photographed a thirty-three-year-old divorced woman sitting on the hood of a parked automobile with two younger friends. She makes the cruising scene every weekend and relies on it as a primary means of socialization.

Clearly, cruising and hanging out are folkloric events of considerable magnitude in the lives of these young people, functioning to decrease the stress created by school and/or work pressures and to release tensions that arise from problems at home and in other interpersonal relationships. Alan Stockard, who grew up along the extreme northeastern margin of Kentucky's Upper Cumberland, recorded some of his recollections about cruising and hanging out. Now a college student and a veteran of the recent Gulf War, Stockard wrote:

What are we doing tonight? This is a question I'd ask a group of friends every Friday night as the weekend fast approached. Growing up in my town didn't afford too many choices, especially for teenagers. The three most-favored things to do were cruising, hanging out, or camping out. Life didn't hold much excitement for us at that age. The fun we had was definitely creative. . . .

The Friday night ritual—cruising—was usually preceded by a football game or basketball game, depending on the season. During the warmer months, anytime was cruising time. Usually what this consisted of was four or five good friends piling into one of our cars and driving around the local hangouts, in my case McDonald's Restaurant and the old Wal-Mart parking lot.

When I first began to "cruise," I was about the age of fourteen. I became friends with someone old enough to drive and we'd take off. The only reason for cruising at this stage was to simply kill time. As my interest in females increased, around the age of fifteen and sixteen, cruising took on a whole different meaning. At that point I was no longer just killing time, I was being "cool." As humorous as it seems now, those cruising days meant everything at the time. I learned a lot about life in the backseat of my buddy's car, things I just had to find out for myself. . . .

"Hanging out" could mean numerous things. Sometimes hanging out would just mean shooting the bull in the local parking lot with my friends. This paralleled with cruising. When cruising got to be too much, you simply pulled in at McDonald's and sat on the hood of your car, talking with just about everybody as the night went on.

The best time for hanging out was after a ballgame. All the local teenagers would gather at the respected times to eat or just be seen. You would either cruise or hang out or vice versa. Another spot to hang out was at a friend's house. Usually if nothing was happening around town, we would gather and watch a few movies into the wee hours of the morning. Although this sounds innocent enough, the night was never complete without "war stories" of each other's girl friends and a few crank calls to our "favorite" teacher, usually about three o'clock in the morning.

Those cruising and hanging out days are long gone now, but the memories I'll cherish forever. To tell you the truth, whenever I'm back in my hometown and when no one's watching, I'll cruise around that infamous route once or twice and have a simple laugh just remembering those days gone by.

Compared to certain daredevil social uses of the automobile by teenagers, cruising is a rather mild recreational activity. For example, the game of "tag" involves tapping the rear bumper of the car ahead while speeding recklessly down the road. "String racing," a game that may be unique to certain Russell County youngsters, occurs as two vehicles tied together by a four- to five-foot cloth string travel at a high rate of speed down the highway. The point of the game is to keep from breaking the string that connects them. Participants swear that if the cord breaks they can tell which vehicle was at fault.

"Chicken," another game that was especially popular during the 1960s (and through the 1970s in some places), was the most dangerous activity engaged in by daredevil teen drivers. Two vehicles would head straight at each other at a high speed, and the driver who lost courage and veered off just in time to avoid hitting the other car head-on was called a "chicken."

Also in the late 1960s, Livingston Academy students, and perhaps others in the region, played the racing game they referred to as "rat racing." Like "chicken," rat racing involved only two cars. However, instead of confronting each other head-on, the two drivers sought to retain the lead position as they raced between two towns. They frequently passed each other at breakneck speed during the open-road contest. The Livingston-to-Celina rat racers did not slow down, even as they crossed over Dale Hollow Dam. Passing took place on the dam

itself, with no more than three to four inches of clearance between the passing vehicle and the concrete railings on the dam. Jim Bowman of Livingston explained that the closer the passing car came to the railings, the braver the driver was thought to be.

Some of today's teen-agers prefer involvement in music to cruising, and their musical tastes run the gamut from old-time country and bluegrass to heavy metal. Students typically prefer one style of music to the exclusion of all others, and often disparage different types, calling rock 'n roll "redneck" and bluegrass and country "country hick" or "dumb." Whatever their musical preference is, students are often consumed by it during nonschool hours. Scotty Garrett and Shane Roberts, who were juniors at Cookeville High School during the 1991–92 academic year, illustrate this degree of interest. Their feelings about and involvement in bluegrass epitomize how a certain segment of high schoolers feel about this music—a genre that has definite roots in old-time music.

Young men who have been string racing between Jamestown and Russell Springs (Photo by the author)

I first met them in May 1991 at the annual Poke Sallet Festival in Gainesboro, to which they had come as participants in the music festivities of the day. Following their appearance on stage with their regular bluegrass band members from Cookeville, including Shane's father, the two young men, guitar cases in hand, sought out a musical jam session already in progress. The event was organized by and featured the Macon County Old-Timers, a group of men middle-aged and older.

Age differences did not bother Scotty and Shane. The two young fellows uncased their guitars and found seats next to the other musicians, who did not view them as "young squirts." They were fellow musicians who readily joined in, loving every minute of it.

Five weeks later, I was in the backroom at the L & M Music Company in Cookeville, documenting a bluegrass jam session that has taken place there every Saturday afternoon since 1982. Except for these two young men and a thirteen-year-old female fiddler, the musicians were middle-aged or older.

There was much joking around. One guitarist asked the mandolin player what key they had just played in. "Was that F or D or me?" he wanted to know.

"I don't know," the serious response came back, "but it was high up there somewhere."

About that time, two more musicians walked through the front door to join the six already there, one of whom commented to me, jokingly, "These two fellows coming here are from Nashville" (implying that they had made the big-time music scene).

Another of the six yelled out, "Did you fellows fly up the interstate to get here on time?"

Before a response could be given, still another laughed aloud at the shorts one of the tall, lanky, late-arrivals was wearing. "Somebody cut off the bottom half of his pants," he yelled.

Informal greetings over, the two newcomers produced their upright bass and rhythm guitar and joined the others in a beautiful interpretation of "Brand New Wagon," a poignant song describing the return home of a native son who found that his parents had died and that the old homeplace, wagon included, was covered with weeds and falling into decay.

During the course of the afternoon, I steered Scotty and Shane aside long enough to talk about their involvement in bluegrass music. Scotty, then sixteen, had been playing lead guitar since he was seven. Shane, also sixteen, began playing rhythm guitar in 1990.

"Why do you like bluegrass music?" I asked the boys.

Shane was first to speak. "I like the beat to it. I like the sound. I like the instruments. They sound a lot better than all these electric guitars and drums." He went on, "I just like it a lot better than that rock 'n roll stuff. The words, the beat, the instrumentation, the lyrics. The words, especially, have more meaning than either rock or country."

Shane knew why he preferred bluegrass music, and he was articulate in its defense. It was obvious that he spoke Scotty's sentiments as well. The only comment Scotty made was to indicate the music he did not like or tolerate. "I like music, period, but I don't care for rock 'n roll or rap," he said.

Scotty and Shane frequently get together to play their music. They admit to singing as well as playing during these informal practice sessions, but "we never sing out [in public]," Scotty commented. Both aspire to continue their involvement with bluegrass after high school, and both would like to turn professional, though they realize how unlikely such an outcome is.

"That's a pretty hard row to hoe," Shane commented.

"Not many make it big," added Scotty, shaking his head all the while.

Country music, especially contemporary country, is also a favorite of many high school students in the Upper Cumberland in the 1990s. However, rock, pop, and alternative music appear to be the most popular listening and participatory music forms among the high school students interviewed.

At the far end of the high school rock music spectrum is a Cookeville heavy metal group known as Black Dawn, comprising Eric Howard, Roger Kumar, Matt Profant, Rob Ray, and Eddie Thompson. At the time I documented them in a practice session all wore shoulder-length hair that provided them with a resemblance to band members in Metallica, Queens Ryche, and Rush, three heavy metal ensembles these guys "grew up on." Black Dawn is continuing a musical tradition that began in the 1950s with rock 'n roll and moved in successive stages through heightened percussive sounds.

Their equipment, including a modest sound system, cost approximately $7,500 and was paid for entirely by the members. Since the emphasis is on loud, pulsating music, Eric the drummer is a vital cog in the band; his hands bounce from cymbals to drums in concert with the bass player and guitarists. When the music is at full crescendo, there is no way to understand the words being sung by Eddie, the vocalist.

Casual listeners might describe this music as harsh and discordant. An informed, appreciative audience, on the other hand, would see the serious expressions on the band members' faces and perceive creativity at work. That's the way these five fellows view their musical performance. "It's an exciting, vibrant music that has a lot of energy to it," noted Roger Kumar.

Howard commented that Black Dawn's sound "is a little heavier and a little more original than other rock bands in this area. The others play well-known stuff. We write a lot of our own.... Our music is complicated. You have to know something about it to understand it. I'm not talking about all kinds of heavy metal, just the kind I like—fast and energetic."

Matt Profant agreed. "We have a more complex music; different time signatures," he said.

Rob Ray observed, "We try to be different. We don't really rock to please people. We rock to please ourselves. Since we're teen-agers, we're full of energy, and this is a real aggressive type of music. It lets our aggressions out by helping us express our creativity."

When I asked the group to identify their typical audience, three or four of them yelled in unison, "Us!!" Rob's father, also present at that mid-summer 1991 practice session held in his home, lifted his hand and smiled in agreement.

Black Dawn performs on occasion for appreciative teen audiences at the Community Center in Cookeville. "It gives us something to do, a place to play," observed Rob. "At the same time it gives others [teen-agers] something to do besides cruising," he continued.

Another music form high schoolers appreciate is rap. Once the exclusive property of black musicians, it is still performed by a couple of all-black groups at Cookeville High. Derived from early African-American music forms, rap is accepted by black students and white students alike, not only as a listener's music but as a performer's. I was surprised to learn of an all-white high school rap group in Livingston, Tennessee (Knights of the Round Table), and one in Albany, Kentucky. When I spoke about this in July 1991 with John Robinson and Robert Gibbs, high school juniors at Sparta, I asked how they felt about white students performing black music. Robinson shrugged it off, commenting that segregation is no longer in vogue in Sparta. "We're all the same," he said, "and we all listen to the same music these days."

These various folkloric activities engaged in by today's adolescents—music-making, slumber parties, campouts, cruising, or other forms of socializing such as hunting and fishing—help them to achieve a personal identity and to bond with others their age. These events help to deepen peer relationships as well as to promote socially sanctioned behaviors that are important in the process of growth toward maturity and adulthood.

7

Social, Generational, and Gender-Bonding Activities

Convivial activities among adults have always been a strong presence in the Upper Cumberland. Many of these continue today in combination with newer forms of socializing and gender-bonding. Men of all ages still hang around country stores; old-timers continue to add flavor and zest to their lives by gathering on the courthouse grounds for a day of whittling while swapping hunting and fishing yarns; knife traders, sportsmen, and other "liars" gather at local restaurants, garages, and service stations to sell and swap wares and exchange stories of every conceivable variety; women commune with each other at homemakers' and cottage prayer meetings, local beauty shops, by telephone and, in some recent instances, during hunting and fishing trips by themselves or in the company of others. Many adults in their middle-to-late years, often with their children, enjoy Saturday nights at community centers scattered across the region listening and dancing to the music of local country rock and bluegrass bands. And older women and men share periods of fellowship, fun, physical activity, and reminiscing at senior citizen centers located in all the counties across the region. By examining some of these folklife forms, we will see that while certain generational and gender roles have remained constant across the years, some functions have changed appreciably with the times.

THE URGE TO TRADE OR SELL

Until the advent of World War II, the first Monday of each month was referred to as Jockey Day or Court Day in most of the county seat towns of the region. On such days matters requiring action by the county and fiscal courts were dealt with, but there was also much drinking, fighting, and visiting taking place on the streets and in the courthouse square.

The term "Jockey Day" was used because of the sale and trade of livestock that transpired at this time. It was not only horses, mules, and cattle being sold or traded but also dogs, knives, pistols, shotguns, farm machinery, and Indian arrowheads.

Many local livestock markets had their beginnings here. By the 1930s it was common practice to organize and charter livestock commission companies. On a set day each week these companies held livestock sales during which farm animals were auctioned off to the highest bidder. The commission company retained a modest fee for care and handling. Local "penhookers" were constant competitors to the livestock commissions, as they remained outside the livestock market building ready to jump onto each truck that pulled up with a cargo of livestock. They attempted to offer owners attractive prices for their animals, while allowing enough margin for a profit when the creatures were run through the sales ring or taken to a larger market miles away and sold there.

The livestock commission companies are still around and command as much attention as ever from farmers in the area, who typically refer to these marketing agencies as "stock pens" or "stock yards." Jockey Day and its attendant activities, however, have been gone since the 1940s. For many area residents, these events were replaced by the yard and garage sales of more recent vintage.

GENDER-BONDING ACTIVITIES

Loafing   The trading of knives and other small items continues apace among older men, many of whom meet daily on the courthouse lawns where they occupy public benches and spend time whittling on pieces of cedar or yellow poplar, spitting tobacco juice into the piles of wooden shavings that grow throughout the day, monitoring activities around the city square, sharing stories of generations past, and talking about local events as recent as yesterday's hailstorm. These activities are not likely to cease in the near future, as county officials in the Upper Cumberland have not taken steps to prevent the old-timers from gathering on the courthouse grounds.

Young and middle-aged males convene daily inside local restaurants, sometimes for biscuits and gravy, but always for coffee and conversation. Their reasons for gathering are varied but typically revolve around knife trading, sharing yarns and boasts about their dogs, hunting, and fishing, or simply recounting recent happenings in the local community. If a humorous twist can be applied to an event, one of the fellows present will find a way to do it. Even the waitresses join in the ribbing. As I watched one young woman pour coffee for the knife traders gathered at a

Whittling and visiting on the Smith County courthouse lawn, Carthage (Photo by the author)

table in Edmonton, I jokingly commented, "So these fellows actually buy something when they come in here!"

"No," she responded with a wink, "just mostly pay rent on the chairs."

A second table across the room was occupied by another group of men who had no apparent bonding agent other than male fellowship. Huddled around still a third table, know by all present as the "liars' bench," were a half-dozen fellows who referred to those gathered at the second table as "beginners." "You have to graduate from that corner before you join the liars' bench," said Dr. Joe Hayes, a liar and dentist.

When I asked the "liars" in a serious vein whether any of them were weekend hunters, Jack Hurt, a gospel singer and auto parts dealer, said, "Naw, I don't hunt; I ain't lost nothing!"

Male socializing takes place at numerous service stations across the Upper Cumberland. A typical example is found at Whitleyville, Jackson County, where four males in their late thirties and early forties were spotted in mid-1991 sitting on folding chairs and milk crates at the back of an old garage. They were sipping beer, just passing the time of day. Talk was better than work, they freely admitted.

"What do you talk about during these sessions—sex?" I jokingly inquired.

"No, no," one of the fellows cackled. "That subject very seldom comes up, as old as we are!"

When the laughter subsided, they commented that hunting and

The general store was and still is a gathering place for area residents, 1973. (Photo by Debbie Gibson)

politics are frequent topics of conversation, as are the game of rolly hole marbles (described below), hornyheads (a freshwater fish), and dryland fish (morels; called murgels in some localities). Perhaps surprisingly, these men had been talking about the death penalty as I drove up. The question they were discussing was not whether there should or should not be a death penalty, but whether they themselves would be able to pull the lever to kill the convicted person. They all agreed that they could not do it, even if the convicted person were indeed guilty of murder.

In early 1992, twenty self-employed males, following such trades as sand hauling, carpentry, plumbing, and wiring, were socializing around coffee and food at a restaurant in Albany before departing for their daily work routines. The only woman present was the waitress. I observed and listened, hoping to discern what bonding agents were at work among these fellows. Eventually, I asked those present at one of the tables what they typically talk about.

The "liars' table," Edmonton (Photo by the author)

Men socializing at a garage, Jackson County (Photo by the author)

"Oh, usually about women, about each other, the things that happened on the job yesterday, and about the town drunks," responded one fellow.

The others laughed in agreement, with one commenting, "You got that right!"

Local women, too, gather in groups at this same restaurant at other times during the day. Included among their topics of conversation, according to Sue Williams, an Albany legal secretary, are the boredom associated with housework, their jobs, unappreciative spouses, former husbands, children, new male friends, flirtations, campouts, and walking for physical fitness.

Rolly Hole Marbles   "What else besides an old-fashioned marble game," writes columnist Byron Crawford of the Louisville *Courier-Journal,* "could reduce grown men to crawling around for hours in the hot sun, on their hands and knees in the dirt, without pay?"

The game of marbles—a three-hole variety—to which Crawford refers is the most unique competitive sport in all the Upper Cumberland and is a distinguishing cultural feature of the region. The game of rolly hole marbles and its legendary kingpin, Dumas Walker of Moss, Tennessee, prompted the song "Dumas Walker," made famous in 1990 by the Kentucky Headhunters, a country rock outfit whose members at that time largely hailed from Metcalfe County.

Rolly hole was never played in all corners of the region; it has been historically centered in the counties of Clay, Jackson, Macon, and Overton in Tennessee, and Adair, Clinton, Cumberland, Metcalfe, Monroe, and Russell across the line in Kentucky. The two most prominent counties involved in rolly hole competition then and now are Clay and Monroe, separated only by the state line on which Dumas Walker's "beer joint" was located. Nor was the name "rolly hole" used to identify the game in all communities even where it was played. It appears that the term originated in the Jackson-Clay area with the likes of Hunter Reecer, Leslie Walker, and Millard Plumlee, all of whom were "old men" when Dumas Walker, who was born in 1915, was just a lad. Because of extensive television and newspaper coverage in recent years referring to the game as "rolly hole," that term eventually replaced the more typical label "marbles." As a child in northern Monroe County who actively participated in the sport, I knew it by the latter designation. "Let's play marbles" was the invitation to engage in this fascinating activity that often consumed an entire day.

Most one-room schools in the area at one time had a marble yard, and many of these were still in operation until the advent of consolidated schools in the 1950s. Whether located on the school grounds or somewhere else in the community, such as in a blacksmith shop in Burristown, Jackson Country, or on the courthouse grounds in Celina, the marble yard used by youngsters was referred to as the "boy's yard," while the men's playground located nearby was known as the "big yard." Dumas Walker, already a "good marble player at the age of eight," was often invited to play in competition with the adults. Walker commented that, in those days, so many adult men were present and waiting their

turn to play that teams typically played only one game and then relinquished the yard to two other teams.

Rolly hole competition normally takes place during daylight hours, although there are reports of fires being built at each end of the marble yard in order to provide adequate light for nighttime matches. The first known person to have a lighted court, around 1948, was black blues musician and marble maker Bud Garrett, then a resident of the Free Hill community overlooking the town of Celina. Power for lighting Garrett's marble yard was provided by a half-dozen Delco batteries.

Wherever it is played, the game of rolly hole marbles provides young fellows an opportunity to emulate their fathers and other older men. Too, the local form of marbles was and still is played in a social environment familiar to those who grew up with rural, agrarian lifestyles and who treasured periods of interaction with friends and neighbors.

Rolly hole is a highly organized, fiercely competitive game of strategy involving two or more players, and has strict, unwritten rules for

Joe Billy Bowman in a game of rolly hole marbles (Photo by the author)

determining the winner. "Furthermore," writes folklore-trained Becky Morse, "it is a game involving complex social interaction and physical skill in a defined context." There are inevitably nonparticipant observers, usually a dozen or so but sometimes in excess of one hundred. Since these onlookers are usually marble players themselves, their presence serves to intensify the verbal interaction between the contestants and heighten the sense of competition.

Rolly hole is played with handmade stone marbles on a smooth, finely packed dirt court. While the marble yard's dimensions may vary slightly from community to community depending on the nature of the terrain, it is typically forty feet long and twenty-four feet wide. The edge of the yard is clearly marked either by the manner in which the surface is groomed or by wooden poles that contain the rectangular playing area. When a marble is knocked out of bounds, it must be shot from behind the line at the point where it went out. The yard contains three holes, each of which is the size of a typical marble. The holes are spaced ten feet apart in a straight line running lengthwise through the center of the yard.

The game can be played by any number of individuals without partners, but the standard contest involves two teams with two players each. The object of the game is for both players on a team to shoot their marbles into all three holes as they move up and down the court three times. In other words, each hole has to "be made" three times by each player while he also assists his partner and keeps the opposing team from making the holes by hitting their marbles and knocking them away.

The game begins with the flipping of a coin to see which team "rolls" first. The first roll is made by each player from behind the first or "bottom hole," as he shoots his marbles toward the middle hole. A person shoots by cradling the stone marble between his down-pointed thumb and the next two fingers. A form of "English" is employed that causes the marble to spin around and around as it makes contact with the ground near the middle hole and moves on toward its destination. When the fourth person has made the initial roll, the first player has the choice of shooting again for the middle hole and then moving on to the next one, or shooting at one or more of the enemy marbles in an effort to knock them away from the hole. If the decision is made to hit an enemy marble, and if contact is indeed made, the shooter then has one bonus shot that can be used either in rolling for the needed hole or placing his marble in some strategic defensive location so as to assist his partner. The object of the game is to keep the other team from making the holes while making one's own in the process.

If a player's marble rolls to within a "span" (distance covered by player's extended hand from thumb to tip of fingers) of the hole he is "for" (the required next hole), he may span to that hole on his next turn and "make" it unless an opposing player hits his marble and knocks it away in the meantime. The span may also be used at anytime during the game each time the player prepares to shoot. Players must not "fudge," however, by covering more distance than a legal span provides. If such a thing happens, contestants or persons on the sideline may yell out an order for the shooter to "knuckle down," i.e., take a legal span and then place the hand holding the marble solidly against the ground at the tip of the span finger.

When a player makes the hole he is for, he wins the opportunity to make one additional play. He may choose to shoot for the next hole, roll to some strategic defensive location on the court, or "lay" (leave the marble in the hole awaiting an opportunity to knock away a marble belonging to the opposing team). Should the player accidentally or intentionally roll his marble into a hole he is not for, he is "dead," thus losing an opportunity to take another shot at that time.

Even if a player's marble is in a hole, an opposing player may make that same hole by rolling his marble onto the top of the one already there. Anytime a player makes a hole or hits an opponent's marble, he is entitled to one additional shot. He can again hit the opponent or "ride him" toward the next-needed hole, but upon the second contact with the same opponent's marble, the shooter is dead until the other three players have taken their turns. However, if the shooter prefers to shoot at the other opponent's marble and successfully makes contact with it, he is still entitled to one more shot. At that point, the shooter decides whether to roll for the next hole, or "die" by hitting that opponent's marble the second time. Thus, by hitting each opponent's marble once, a player may have three shots in succession.

If a player hits his partner's marble, knocking it toward the needed hole, he is dead. But if he "glances" off the partner's marble and hits an opponent's marble in the process, he has one additional shot coming. Both the partner and the opponent must begin their next shot from the points at which their marbles came to rest.

Dumas Walker and Welby Lee, the latter of Tompkinsville, who often played as partners in marble games from the 1950s through the 1970s, were the acknowledged best shots in the region when it came to hitting their opposition's marbles. Walker himself commented about their prowess: "Me or Webb Lee wouldn't miss more than one marble out of a hundred if that fellow's marble wasn't any farther away than eleven feet."

The process involved in making the stone marbles used in the game of rolly hole is as interesting and challenging as the game itself. Limestone and other types of rock have been used for making marbles, but flint, by far the most preferred, is all that is used nowadays. The first step in making a flint marble is to search area hillsides and ledges in quest of the best grades of red, black, or white flint rocks, white being the most common variety. The less stratified the chunks of flint, the less likely the finished marbles are to burst open when struck time and again by other flint marbles.

Up through my own childhood years in the late 1930s and early 1940s, the rough flint was broken into pieces approximately one-fourth the size of a clenched fist. The maker would then hold the piece of flint in one hand and strike it with a metal file or chisel with the other, hewing the stone into a round form considerably larger than the marble it would turn into. By the time the chipped edges of the stone were smoothed, however, its future form would begin to be apparent.

The smoothing process was accomplished by means of a whirligig (spinning handtool) during the nineteenth century and early years of the twentieth. Bud Garrett felt that Lawrence Rich of Baptist Ridge in Clay County, who made flint marbles into the 1980s, was the last of the old-time craftsmen to employ the whirligig in marble making.

With the introduction of bicycles and automobiles into the region in the 1920s, it soon became standard practice to employ the wheels of these vehicles to smooth the marbles, a process locally referred to as "grinding." Using a bicycle involved turning it upside down, with one person turning the pedals by hand. Having carved into an emery rock a hole just large enough to hold the marble, a second person would hold the marble against the rotating bike tire. The marble was smoothed as it turned around and around inside the emery.

Since bicycles were luxuries that most families could not afford until after 1945, automobile or truck wheels were commonly employed for grinding marbles. A rear wheel would be jacked up and safely secured with rocks and blocks of wood placed underneath the axle. With the transmission in neutral so as to allow the suspended wheel to turn freely, a person would then place one end of a tobacco stick into the wheel spokes and turn the wheel at a brisk pace while a co-worker would hold the grindstone containing the rough-hewn flint marble against the spinning rubber wheel. (This is what my brother Charles and I were doing in late 1939 when our baby sister Madeline came out to investigate the specialists in action. Just as she crept within a few inches of the turning wheel, the tobacco stick slipped and struck her across the forehead, sending her reeling backwards, unconscious. As fate would have it, my mother stepped to the door at that very instant. She began shrieking, "You've killed my baby! You've killed my baby!" We hadn't, but I surely thought at the time that we had.)

Once the grinding stage was finished, a new hole was chiseled into the side of the emery. The marble and the stone that cradled it were placed under running water so that the marble inside the hole would be rotated until the surface had a slick, glassy surface. After about two weeks of this, the marble, now approximately three-fourths of an inch in diameter, was ready to be entered into competition.

Bud Garrett, acknowledged master at marble making, claimed that in almost fifty years of producing flint marbles, he knew of only two of his products that had "busted" in play. He replaced both of them free of charge, as his policy was to guarantee his marbles for the lifetime of the purchaser.

Most people made marbles for personal use and still treasure the ones that are left. They were sometimes made for sale, however, and still are. Garrett recalled selling one red flint marble for thirty-five dollars in 1935 and another made from the same rock for twenty-five dollars that year. At that time, his standard price for handmade marbles (made with a grindstone mounted on a stand and without the benefit of the water-polishing process) ranged between one and five dollars. (In more recent times on up until his death in 1988, Garrett's standard price for marbles made with a power-turned grinder varied from five to fifteen dollars.) He made and sold enough marbles in the mid-1940s so that he was able to purchase for $1,500 a ten-year-old-Clay County school bus, which he used as a daily shuttle to haul residents of Free Hill to and from work in Celina. After dropping his passengers off each morning, Garrett took his marble-making rig from the bus and spent all day there in Celina making new marbles or smoothing surfaces on old ones that had been "fleeked" (chipped) during a marble game. Today at any marble game it is still possible to purchase a handmade specimen from persons who attend primarily to sell their power-turned products that can be made on the spot in a couple of hours.

Adult males have been fascinated by the game all along. Some school-age boys have manifested renewed interest in the sport in recent times, as evidenced by their involvement in Standing Stone State Park's National Rolly Hole Championship, held annually since the mid-1980s, and their presence as competitors at occasions such as the celebration in June 1991 marking Mammoth Cave National Park's fiftieth anniversary —an event that involved teen-age and adult marble players from Rock Bridge and Center Point in Monroe County.

In April 1992, the Tennessee-Kentucky Sharpshooters, comprising six factory worker/farmer rolly hole marble players from Clay and Monroe counties, were flown to England to compete in the British Marble Championship and the World Championship. These contestants from the Upper Cumberland (Kentuckians Ron Branstetter and Bobby

A father instructs his son in rolly hole marbles, Celina, Tennessee. (Photo by the author)

Dyer and Tennesseans Travis Cherry, Russell Collins, Junior Strong, and Jack Tinsley) returned home with both championship trophies, winning ten games while losing none.

In typical marble-player fashion, a Clay County shooter said of the victors, "Aw, they was just lucky; the best players didn't even go over there!"

Various individuals in the Cumberland River country continue to build and maintain marble yards as places where friends come to socialize around this very competitive game. Those present continue the decades-old tradition of arguing over who has the best marble, who is the best marble shooter around, who fudges the most, and other friendly but all-consuming arguments that, if resolved, would take much of the fun out of the game.

Cockfighting   Cockfighting and drag racing are male-dominated sports common to the region. The latter is a widespread activity that hardly needs describing here; I will only mention that it still takes place regularly near Monticello in Kentucky and at Crossville and Buffalo Valley (Putnam County) in Tennessee. Cockfighting, on the other hand, is somewhat more esoteric and exotic. Still illegal in Tennessee but officially sanctioned in Kentucky since 1981, cockfights in the Upper Cumberland were once held in backyards and in the back rooms of booze joints. Now, however, unmarked barns and other rural arenas afford ideal spaces for this tense activity that eventually leads to victory or death in the pit.

Cockfighting, an ancient practice in world cultures, has been around the Upper Cumberland for over a century, perhaps since the early days of settlement. Repulsive to most area residents, this activity nonetheless serves as a "rallying point for an entire system of social interaction, group identifications,... social values, and self-representation," says Steven Del Sesto. Cockfights are highly charged folk events that provide participants with organized means of displaying and emphasizing social, symbolic, and psychological conditions and feelings.

Dowell Wallace of Albany, a real estate broker, furniture store owner, and taxicab driver, produces gamecocks and also provides a barn called the Albany Game Club, where fights are staged every second Sunday afternoon. The Clinton County Game Club is Wallace's only local competition. Although these fellows raise some roosters, the largest local producer of game birds is located east of Albany in Duvall Valley, where there are about eight hundred birds at any one time. A good fighting rooster sells for about two hundred dollars, while number-one brood gamebirds bring from eight hundred to two thousand dollars each.

Wallace has operated a cockfighting arena since about 1964. He was raided by local and state police only once, in 1977 while the activity was still illegal. "The troopers closed us down," Wallace recalled.

In a single afternoon of activity, between forty and sixty individual rooster fights will be staged. The owners pay no fee to enter their roosters into competition. The only remuneration Wallace receives is a door fee of five dollars per spectator, which generates a total revenue of between four hundred and five hundred dollars. Some of this money is subsequently paid to the three or four referees employed to see to it that the rules of the fight are strictly followed. The gamecocks' owners position their birds directly on the assigned lines so that they are facing each other, ready for combat. This is called "toeing the line." The referee assumes a position on his knees, a stance he will keep as he maneuvers quickly from one spot to another so as to keep track of everything the roosters do.

The owners of the two combatants stay out of the fenced combat area, called a pit, but remain close by in case the referee calls out

Many gamecocks are
raised in Duvall Valley,
Clinton County.
(Photo by the author)

"Handle!" This command signifies that one or both of the cocks have
hung their steel spurs into the flesh of the other and cannot continue
fighting. The owners have only twenty seconds to plunge into the
gamecock pit and unhang the creatures. If these bloody encounters are
not fatal but drain the cocks' energy so that they become sluggish in
combat, they are removed from the main pit and placed in hollowed-out
"drag pits" where they continue fighting until one kills the other.

Owners, trainers, pit operators, and spectators alike refer to gamecock fights as sporting events. "It's kinda like fishing or hunting or
something like that," Wallace observed. "It's just like you have a dog out
there hunting, and you think yours is just a little bit better than anybody
else's."

In describing the typical reactions of those persons who watch the
fights, Wallace used a ballgame for comparison. "They'll holler and yell,
and they'll talk to the rooster they're for. That's how they act." He went
on to say that the audience usually comprises teachers, lawyers, and
numerous other professional types. About one out of six of those present
is female, married to or dating one of the men present. Those who
frequent the Albany Game Club are from as far away as Indiana, Ohio,
Virginia, and Alabama. "It's a kind of social gathering for a lot of nice
people," Wallace concluded.

***Hunting and Fishing Activities and Converging
Gender Roles***   The Upper Cumberland is a land of low mountains, rugged hills, plateaus, deep valleys, river and creek bottomlands,

and rolling farmlands. The fact that the region is, in places, less developed than most adjacent areas makes it a veritable paradise for hunting and fishing, activities that nowadays attract both men and women. There is a bountiful supply of whitetail deer, wild turkey, and dove, some wild boar, and numerous species of small game, such as groundhogs, that are shot at for sport from the windows of pickup trucks. Fish are plentiful in the area's numerous lakes and streams.

Deer is the game most popular with area hunters, but wild boar hold a particular fascination for some who periodically visit lodges on the Cumberland Plateau. Boar may not be as formidable as grizzlies or as awe-inspiring as mountain lions, but they are "big, mean, fleet of foot and full of fight." They are, in the words of sportswriter H. Lea Lawrence, "easily the most dangerous animal in the eastern United States and their potential to do damage to man and dog alike is extremely high."

I was present at the Clarkrange Hunting Preserve in March 1992, when five huntsmen from Louisville returned to the lodge at the end of a hunt with the carcasses of two boar and two rams in tow. Workers at the lodge immediately set about to get the animals skinned and stored inside the walk-in cooler. The visiting hunters stood shivering in the cold, frosty air, guns and bows in hand, gloating over their kills, ribbing each other about missed shots and narrow escapes, and jokingly calling each other profane names while excitedly watching the skins being ripped from the dead animals.

Lodge owner and operator John Gilbert, after observing the number of gunshots fired at the animals, instructed the hunters to go to the lodge where he would join them shortly and preside over a kangaroo court. "For every guilty charge against a hunter, two inches will be cut off his shirttail," Gilbert announced.

During court proceedings, Gilbert explained that this practice was begun in an effort "to keep hunters from just taking 'sound shots,'" i.e., shooting at anything and everything that made a noise. He went on in a mock-serious voice, "It only takes *one* shot to kill a boar.

"Now I'm going to read a few verses from the scriptures here; this is *The Hunter's Encyclopedia*." [Reads a description of the wild boar.] "Okay, who killed the first boar?" he asked.

"I did, sir," responded the oldest member of the hunting group, user of a muzzle-loading gun.

"Okay, approach the bench. Put your hand on the book. Do you swear to tell the truth, the whole truth, and nothing but the truth, so help you Daniel Boone and Davy Crockett?"

"Yes, your honor."

"How many shots did you fire at your boar?" Gilbert asked.

"Two and a half," responded the accused hunter.

Deer hunters congregate near the Cumberland River in eastern Monroe County. (Photo by the author)

"You shot its leg off with one of your shots," Gilbert charged.

"No-o-o-o-o, your honor. The first shot was a shot! But the second one just went, 'P-o-o-o-o-h-h.' I didn't have enough powder..."

"That's what we call going off half-cocked!" Gilbert charged, as he interrupted the speaker.

"...in the barrel," the accused went on. "But my third shot was with a .44 Magnum."

"And you blowed it in two," Gilbert retorted. "Its neck fell off when I skinned the hide down. And you shot its leg in two! That poor boar would have had to drop [dead] just like a bucket of walnuts."

"How about it, fellows?" asked Judge Gilbert. "Has he been doing his part of the work here at the lodge?"

"Yes, your honor, he's okay there," one of the other hunters yelled back.

"How about air pollution?" inquired the judge. "Did he let a sulphur fart or anything?"

"I did smell something," yelled a hunter.

"That was my muzzle loader," claimed the accused in defense of himself.

"No, no," yelled out another hunter, "that wasn't no muzzle loader."

The accused hunter surrendered with the words, "I'm throwing myself on the mercy of the court. I'm getting old."

"Then how do you plead?" asked the judge. "Shooting too many times?"

"Yes, that and air pollution. I'm guilty."

The judge reached for the hunter's shirttail and proceeded to cut out a two-inch section to be posted on the wall for all to see. Just as he finished, one of the other hunters yelled out, "Hey, judge, reach around there and cut that other thing off, too. Hell, he's too old to use it anyway!"

Two additional trials took place on the spot, with similar verbal exchange and surrendered portions of shirttails. That done, the "judge" departed the scene, leaving the hunters by themselves to prepare the evening meal at the lodge, pull pranks on each other, tell a few racist jokes, and even recount some morale-building stories designed to boost the spirits of those whose hunt had not been too successful. They all agreed that these periodic hunts were eagerly anticipated because of the overall sport of it, the thrill of the kill, the meat itself, and male camaraderie.

Local deer hunters seldom go to these hunting preserves, according to Caroll C. Harvill of nearby Monterey. "Cee," as he is called by his friends, said that "in order to hunt around here you have to either own the land or lease it." Verbal consent from the landowner is sufficient, continued Harvill, who is a member of the Calfkiller Hunting Club, named for the nearby river valley located primarily in White County. The Calfkiller Club leases two thousand acres of land for hunting purposes. Its eighteen members all pay annual membership dues of $156.

Like other hunting and fishing clubs in the Upper Cumberland, this one has instituted bylaws that forbid the drinking of alcoholic beverages on the premises. "You can't mix firearms with alcohol," Harvill said. "Lots of people can't handle it, and they just open up and shoot at anything they see."

"Why do you hunt?" I asked him.

"Me and my brothers and everybody else around here was just raised up to hunt," he responded. "It keeps you out of trouble, and I like the woods. I'd just as soon be in the woods as right here," he went on. "We eat the food, and what we have left over we give to the elderly."

Most contemporary hunters of the Upper Cumberland, both male and female, hunt with rifles, muzzle-loading guns, and bows. The latter

A hunter loses his
shirttail for violating the
hunting codes.
(Photo by the author)

two have been much in vogue since the late 1970s, which was about the
same time that certain forms of hunting, especially deer, became popular
with women as well as men. Typically, if the husband and father hunt
(and approximately 70 percent of them do), so do wives and children.
Cee's wife hunts; their nineteen-year-old son has hunted since he was
eight; their daughter, Sherrie, twenty, has killed three deer; and their
nineteen-month-old granddaughter, when asked jokingly how many deer
she had killed, quickly responded, "Two," as she held up two fingers.
When asked how she had killed the deer, the child fired back, "Bam!
bam!"

Hunting is truly a family matter with the Harvills, a tradition that has
been unbroken since family progenitors moved to the Hanging Limb-
Monterey area many decades ago. The early Harvill generations walked
or rode horseback to the site of their hunt; today, family members
employ all-terrain vehicles, typically called "four-wheelers."

Deer hunting in earlier years involved the use of hounds, a practice
seldom employed today. When a deer passed close enough to the hunter,
a shot would ring out that could be heard for great distances. Then the
hunter's voice told others what to expect with such exclamations as, "I
missed," "I got it," or "It won't go far." These same outbursts are
popular today.

Like the men, many women of the Upper Cumberland are activity-
oriented. They hunt for the same reasons men do, enjoying to the fullest
any and all challenges associated with this enterprise. Regarding her first
deer kill, Margaret Cope of Bon Air, White County, described the feeling

as being "like Christmas and the Easter rabbit and your birthday and New Year's Eve" all at the same time. Nancy Wells of Burkesville commented that she felt like "king of the mountain"—that she could not have been any higher. Libby Anderson of Marrowbone said, "The adrenalin started going and I was so nervous!" Sherrie Harvill recalled an intense "sense of pride" that swept over her the moment she realized her quest was complete.

These four women, along with Kathy Tupman of Jamestown, Kentucky, and Melissa Wells, daughter of Nancy Wells, were all interviewed in connection with their hunting activities. The six women subjects varied in age from twenty to forty-five, in hunting experience from one time only up to twelve years, and in success at bagging a deer from none to eight. Four of these women were married; the two singles were progeny of hunting mothers.

According to Margaret Cope, today's women hunters typically begin the sport in company with a father, husband or boyfriend. Although four of the six subjects made their decisions to hunt without being specifically encouraged to do so by a man, all were motivated and challenged by the activities of a father or husband who hunted. Sherrie Harvill, who began to hunt with her father at age ten, told of being so excited the night before that she often went to bed with her hunting clothes on for fear she would not wake up in time to get dressed.

Nancy Wells, a teacher and mother, admitted to having mixed emotions when her husband first asked her to go hunting with him. There were things that needed to be done around the house, she said,

Cee Harvill and his daughter, Sherrie, with hunting equipment (Photo by the author)

but she agreed to go hunting with her husband so they could spend time together. Like Nancy Wells, Libby Anderson decided to begin hunting so that she and her husband, who felt the necessity to hunt for the meat it afforded the family, could be together more.

When Margaret Cope and Kathy Tupman announced to their husbands that they intended to join them on a hunt, their spouses were supportive. Tupman stated that she began deer hunting so as to experience the excitement of getting "the big one."

Women of the Upper Cumberland hunt alone or with fathers, husbands, boyfriends, or a female companion. Two of the women interviewed have hunted with men other than their husbands. Margaret Cope explained, "Now, I had to be careful who I went with. I couldn't just call anybody and say, 'Hey, do you want to go hunting today?' All wives don't understand." She went on, "The fact that you've got on forty-two layers of clothes [smothered with] skunk scent or doe pee says there's nothing else going on. You're going to the woods to *hunt*, folks!"

Some women clean their own guns; in other cases, men do it for them. Cope admitted that her husband cleans her gun at times, then added, "I wash his underwear! So it's like this, if he wants clean underwear, sometimes he can clean my gun."

The gender difference is clear when the time comes to field-dress the slain deer. Women express their difficulty in performing the task; some say that they just cannot do it. All except one commented that the offensive smell when the carcass is gutted is the worst single factor in the unpleasant process. However, the mark of a real female hunter is not participation in field-dressing the deer but her ability to make the kill.

The question of feminism inevitably enters the picture, even though most women hunters do not expressly think along these lines. Tupman openly defended the traditional woman's role by commenting, "I'm very old-fashioned. A woman's place is taking care of the children first of all, doing the cooking and cleaning and ironing. And the man's place is to be out doing 'Honey, do this; honey, do that' jobs."

While insistent that she was not expressing any kind of women's independence, Margaret Cope seemingly challenged the traditional gender roles practiced by Upper Cumberland residents. "I think we found out that we could do whatever we wanted to," Cope commented. "Girls are brought up [to think] 'Look, you're a girl, you're supposed to do these things.' . . . Those of us who are of our own mind got to a point where we realized that, hey, we didn't make these rules, we don't have to live by them."

In spite of the respect women hunters have earned from their male counterparts, jokes are told about their entry into this previously all-male bastion. Cee Harvill, a highly respected hunter himself and a father and husband who taught the female members of his family the art of hunting, hesitantly shared a story sometimes told in local male circles about women deer hunters and their presumed lack of knowledge:

> This woman never had been hunting before, and she kept on her husband to take her hunting. So he went down and bought her a new gun, orange vest, and clothes to take with her. He went out and set her on this ridge that morning. He went two ridges over.
>
> In about an hour, he heard her shooting two or three times. So he walked back over there where she was and there stood a game warden [over] a dead horse. She told him she was getting her deer and taking it home. The game warden said, "If you'll just give me a chance to get my saddle off [the deer], you can have it!"

Real joking and pranking may occur when a female hunter's peers decide to take matters into their own hands. Sometimes their actions reflect an opposition to the killing of animals for whatever reason; at other times they simply enjoy teasing those who hunt for sport. Such was the case when Kathy Tupman's fellow office workers at Lake Cumberland Lodge decided to "aggravate" her on the occasion of her first hunt. She related the following:

> Well, I'm kinda a prankster myself around the office, so they have to get back at me. "You couldn't shoot a poor, little deer," they said.
>
> I said, "Yes, I can."
>
> They decided they was gonna fix me up at my deer stand. I kinda suspicioned something, . . . so I went to my deer stand to check it out. That was on a Friday afternoon, and deer season started the next morning. I decided I'd better go down to my deer stand and check it out, see if these girls had fixed me up with anything.
>
> Well, I went down there and I said, "Tony! Come here and look." I could see all kinds of stuff hanging on my deer stand. They had took this big, huge pair of panties—I mean two or three of me could fit into them!
>
> See, they had always teased me and told me that if I shot at a deer, that I'd use the bathroom in my pants and I'd better take spares along. So they had these big, huge panties up there hanging on the stand. And they left a roll of toilet paper hanging there . . . in case I shot one.

Once the kill has been made and the fresh meat has been cared for, Upper Cumberland deer hunters of both genders enjoy sitting around and talking about the hunt. The chief topics of concern include a description of "how the animal was coming in"—whether it was fast or slow, whether it stopped when the hunter whistled at it in order to have a good shot. They also talk about the kill itself and why some animals become legendary in storytelling sessions.

Nancy Wells recounted the traditional story of Red Top, a very large animal that was talked about by her husband's father and his hunting friends and is still popular with area hunters:

> This Virginia red deer called Red Top was the biggest deer that anyone had ever seen back in the woods. Story has it that the deer was always running when anyone saw it. And it has even been told that it snagged someone's coat as it went by.
>
> This one guy decided that he would slow this deer down. And so he decided that he would string a piece of rope where it always ran by, and he did. But the deer just ran right through the rope and went on.
>
> As far as I know, it was never killed.

Such stories are told when hunters get together in mixed-gender groupings throughout the year to eat wild game, including venison, quail, rabbit, and fish, and to recount their hunting and fishing exploits. Sherrie Harvill laughingly commented that, at these social gatherings, the deer sometimes become bigger than they actually were.

Most hunters have a deep and abiding respect for the creatures they hunt. Cee Harvill provided the following description of an old deer, reminiscent of Red Top, that helps to explain why he and other hunters feel as they do about them:

> I will tell you about one deer that I hunted for almost ten years. He was just too smart. He started out as a 10-pointer—a big, big, deer. I never could get a shot at him. I called him Old Lucky.
>
> That old deer taught us a lot of stuff—how to hunt, how still to be for him, the way to come in on him. We killed a lot of deer by what he taught us.

Historian Larry Whittaker, who grew up east of Cookeville, described the aura that often surrounds both the hunter and the hunted:

> There's very little bragging about hunting. It's almost like everybody is equal. They'll tell about how they hunted a particular deer, this big buck that was kindly legendary in this geographical area.
>
> Sometimes they give the deer names. "I saw Old-So-and-So's tracks down here." They'll get very excited about seeing his tracks or what have you. What it amounts to is the hunters joining forces against the deer. But the deer is not an enemy, rather a respected foe. Thus, it's like, "We don't want to kill the deer because we hate him; we want to kill him because we admire him."
>
> Then the person who finally gets the deer is like a hero. Not because he's a superior hunter; he was just lucky and happened to be the one who bagged the

deer. Then he sits around and tells how he killed the deer. The others ask him how he killed the deer, and you hear the story over and over and over again about how he stalked the deer, where he shot the deer, and in what part of the body.

I remember standing around the campfire and drinking coffee as a young man. Really, you felt so good doing that that it didn't matter whether you shot a deer or not. In other words, I was with my father and other elders there and we were in a common pursuit. It was like coming of age, a father-son bonding thing.

In earlier times, and perhaps as late as the 1950s, the killing of one's first deer was celebrated in some portions of the region by a ritual process known as "blooding." This significant event, to quote Whittaker, was "a sort of rite of passage. Other hunters 'blood you' when they are field-dressing the deer. They take out the liver and smear the hunter with that."

The same ritualized behavior was practiced by numerous American Indian tribes who, according to folklorist Francis E. Abernathy, typically applied the slain animal's blood between the young hunter's eyes "for good vision, on his legs and arms for strong running and good aim, and above the breast bone for good lungs." In East Texas and adjacent portions of Louisiana, the blood is smeared on the initiate's face only. The ritual appears to have a twofold purpose; first, when the young hunter is smeared with the blood of the animal he has killed, he acquires the vitality and strength necessary to aid in the survival of his hunting group; second, the blood-smearing attests to the fact that the boy has become a man who is able to provide meat for his own family's table.

Blooding is no longer practiced in the Upper Cumberland, and most modern-day hunters are not familiar with the ritual. A hunting event these days has a threefold purpose: sport, socializing, and meat for the family table.

Gender-Bonding among Area Females Women in the Upper Cumberland engage in a number of activities that allow for female bonding, including a limited amount of socializing on the job, getting together in church-related activities, participating in physical fitness programs, and talking at local restaurants and bars. These are important times, especially for working women who have the double burden of keeping up the home front as well.

The social life of the working woman consists largely of having coffee or lunch with friends at work or walking with them after work. Lunch breaks with male friends are typically filled with conversation about job-related topics; with female companions, there is dialogue of a more personal nature. The women share recipes and household tips and talk about their spouses, their jobs, how their children are doing in school, the family budget, church, housekeeping chores, and their own personal feelings and desires. One woman commented that a common topic for her and her friends is husbands who do not appear to understand the strain of working full-time and still being responsible for running the household.

A female church-goer nearing middle age commented that many working women choose to socialize through church activities, especially gender-specific prayer groups. Men are not welcome at these meetings; women are totally in charge. During the course of the event, the women share problems they are having or some of their friends are having, so that the group may pray for them. Marital problems appear to be the favorite topic of conversation. Or, if a mother is having problems with a rebellious child, she provides details to the others present so that they may be able to pray more effectively. The woman who has an unbelieving husband, or whose husband is not as spiritual as he should be, will find sympathetic ears for her concern over her husband's spiritual well-being. Though the problems are discussed at length, few are actually prayed about. Seen in this light, it might be thought that these women are engaging in a restricted form of gossip that is justified by the ostensible religious nature of the gathering.

Women participating in these bonding activities frequently employ narrative structures when describing personal matters. Their stories may be amazing, amusing, or even horror-filled. These narrations "provide a major form of human discourse," says folklorist Susan Johnstad. Narratives pertaining to pregnancy, labor, and childbirth are favorite topics, since women enjoy sharing their personal experiences with others who know about such things on a firsthand basis. Women especially depend upon such sharing of stories because, having historically been denied a voice at the institutional level, "they are able through consciousness raising to affirm and construct who they are and what they want to become," Johnstad continues. Narrative sessions help these women to establish a present identity, a means for coping with life's realities, and assistance in constructing for themselves a world in which they can live.

Some mothers become involved in their children's school activities, such as clubs, for which they may become sponsors, or sports, which requires driving the kids to practice and attending athletic contests, situations that are themselves opportunities for bonding with other parents.

Socializing for many working women takes place on the job, but this is not the case for those who are lone employees or who work only with men. In Albany, five middle-aged women who live alone because of divorce or separation socialize as a group in a local or area restaurant at dinnertime virtually every night of the year. During summer months they go on overnight campouts where they engage in vigorous hiking activities while conversing about the events of the day and week, their children, and their mutual concerns. Like most women in modern cultures everywhere, these five are able through a strong personal support system to share one another's problems and moments of victory. In the words of one, "I couldn't have made it through my divorce had it not been for my friends who listened and consoled me. I treasured their advice."

Social Activities at Community Centers　Persons who have not participated in or at least witnessed firsthand the spirited gatherings that take place at community centers on weekends have no idea how important such affairs are to the 150 or more who do attend. The local music ensembles, such as Country Cookin', Lonesome Travelers, Country Express, Ramblin' Rose, and Big Chiefs, who play for these occasions are typically active every weekend. Some of their music, such as country rock, like some of the dance forms—for example, the twist— are fairly recent additions to the music and dance scene in the Upper Cumberland. But this sort of get-together resembles older folklore genres that have been around for decades.

Every county in the region has one or more locations that serve in this capacity, whether they are called community centers, community clubs, or hunters' clubs or are simply barns or sheds located on private property. Most of these places prohibit the sale of alcoholic beverages as well as the bringing in of bottles. Any drinking that takes place is done outside the building, either in parked vehicles or out of sight behind them. Parents thus have no qualms about taking their small children along for an evening of entertainment. These little ones may dance with a parent or keep company with other children of the same age.

Seldom are black residents of the area present at these events. The musicians, dancers and watchers are almost exclusively white. This is not to say that blacks are not welcome; they probably would be. Judd Anders of Burkesville was a black guitarist and vocalist with Country Cookin' for many years and generally received credit for the overflow crowds that turned out whenever the group performed. The same was true with The Cribbeans, an integrated dance band from the Celina-Burkesville-Tompkinsville area in the 1960s that comprised marble-playing Bud Garrett on electric guitar, Leroy Monk, a black drummer, Merrill Tooley, a white lead guitarist, Benny Williams, a white bass player, and James Graves, a white guitarist. These fellows frequently played for dances and shows over a six-county area before finally calling it quits.

At these present-day community center events, people of all ages engage in various dance movements, including the ballroom variety often

People of all ages at a Saturday night community dance in Mt. Herman, western Monroe County (Photo by the author)

referred to locally as "belly rubbing," the rock 'n roll twist, square dance, and flatfoot (also called heel-and-toe or buck-and-wing dance). The featured music group, while perhaps preferring its own genre, accommodates a wide range of dance preferences by mixing things up and playing to satisfy the choices of everyone present at least a couple of times each evening. Most of the dancers head for the floor every time the music begins, even if that particular dance is not their preference. They manage to create some form of body movement that, at least to them, appears to be perfectly appropriate.

Some of the dancers present are regular members of clogging troupes that may occasionally perform a couple of square-dance sets at the community centers on any given night. More typically, however, the cloggers stage shows for nursing home residents, fund-raising events, and other special functions sponsored by nonprofit organizations. If the purpose of a show is to raise money for the sponsor, a performance fee is levied by the cloggers, but the honorarium is often donated back to the person or group for whom the benefit is staged. If the money is not returned to the benefactor on the spot, the dance troupe typically uses it to purchase inexpensive gifts for nursing home residents or similar other needy people in the area.

There are perhaps a dozen clogging outfits scattered across the Upper Cumberland, most of which have been active for less than twenty years. Although clogging derives from older folk dance forms, it is not itself a part of the region's heritage. Clog dancing features both individual and group performance, often calling for elaborate routines by the colorfully dressed participants. Square dancing, a more traditional form of recreation that derives from British and French antecedents, features dance couples as the basic unit; responding to the instructions of a "caller," they move about in fixed geometric patterns. While both square dancing and clogging are popular in the region, the latter is fast becoming a tradition and promises to leave behind a wide, easy-to-follow trail.

The Country Hoedowners in action at Summer Shade, Kentucky, 1992 (Photo by the author)

One of these groups, the Country Hoedowners, was formed in 1976 by four individuals who "just enjoyed getting together and dancing," said Yema Harlow, a founding member. The four continued to meet and began talking with their friends about the fun of dancing. Their numbers grew and they soon began performing for nursing homes and benefits, where they were always warmly received. Today the group comprises about four dozen adult members and some children from Barren, Cumberland, and Monroe counties. Group members dress alike in red-and-white outfits, men in red shirts and white trousers, women in white blouses and red skirts with full can-can slips and pantaloons underneath.

The Country Hoedowners get together often for fellowship at picnics, potlucks, and other social functions. They meet to dance bimonthly at the Nobob Clubhouse in eastern Barren County, about one mile from the Barren-Monroe border. During the first years of the group's existence, they met to practice before each public performance. But now, said Wayne McCoy in a May 1992 feature story in *The Monroe County Citizen*, "we're so busy dancing that we're always in step."

Senior citizen centers, which are not unique to the Upper Cumberland, provide older area residents with opportunities for socializing that would stagger the imaginations of previous generations. These federally subsidized centers were instituted in 1973 to serve Title VII nutritional needs. At least one center was established in each county throughout the region, sometimes more when local interest justified it. A special transportation program for the aged was made available in each county in 1974, so that the centers are readily accessible to all seniors.

Many different activities take place at these centers, beginning around 8:30 A.M. with the early arrivers and continuing, with official interruptions from time to time, through lunch and often until late afternoon.

Other than quilting, which appears to involve only women, virtually all activities attract both men and women, often in mixed-gender configurations. Those who gather at the Pickett County Community Center in Byrdstown, for example, play rook, hearts, and poker, along with another card game that the locals call "pig." It is strictly subregional, they say, and is largely unknown even in nearby Albany, Cookeville, Crossville, and Livingston.

The seniors at the Pickett center frequently hold one or more informal song sessions during the day, accompanied by a pianist, a guitarist, or both. Their repertoire includes "only the old songs," says one of the participants.

Those who prefer strenuous activities and are physically able to participate go outside the building to engage in popular sports such as pitching horseshoes or playing gender-specific basketball. The same is

true at other senior centers in Tennessee's Upper Cumberland, and once each year those persons involved in basketball and other sports congregate at Tennessee Technological University in Cookeville for Senior Olympics Day.

Obituary columns in daily and weekly local newspapers reveal that people have been living much longer in recent years. Some who presently frequent area senior centers will most likely be around to welcome into their ranks persons who have only recently begun to admit they have reached their middle years. When today's pre-teens and teenagers arrive at the middle stage of life and replace those who, by then, will be seniors, all groups will be viewed as important custodians of regional heritage—all that is good about the folklore and folklife of the historic Upper Cumberland.

Seniors enjoying a game of pig at the community center, Byrdstown (Photo by the author)

The cultural landscape that once reflected an older, family-based agricultural way of life in the Upper Cumberland is quickly slipping away. Numerous old family homes, barns, and other outbuildings reminiscent of earlier life and times stand empty, often rotting away on their foundations. Some of these houses, prestigious from the 1840s to the 1950s, are partially obscured by the newer ranch-type homes or trailers standing in front of them. Barns and cribs have been superceded by prefabricated metal storage sheds and silos.

Generational continuity of land ownership and farming pursuits is still in evidence on some farmsteads across the region. However, many present owners of the land and of historic structures now live in the county seat towns or in distant cities, choosing to lease their property to neighbors or corporate farmers. Absentee ownership is typical in river and creek bottom areas, where as many as three, four, or five older, once stately two-story structures may be standing in advanced stages of decay. Yet the fields surrounding them contain the lessee's lush green crops of hay, corn, and other grains and the hills encircling the stream bottoms provide grazing cattle with more than ample feed.

Rail fences that years ago served to keep animals from straying from their pasturelands now appear only when homeowners use them to decorate lawns. And the rolls of hay that presently dot the landscape during haying seasons have replaced the older rectangular bales and the haystacks that were once common during harvest season.

Modern road construction, designed to complement both service-oriented industry and official tourism activities essentially new to the region, provides still another form of change that is daily altering the landscape. Numerous older homesteads situated along curved roads, though perhaps still occupied by the progeny of nineteenth-century residents, are no longer visible to travelers who speed along the newly straightened arteries. Visitors to the Upper Cumberland might be well advised to traverse the region with county highway maps in hand. Replete with identifying labels such as Old Ky 90 or Old US 127, these important documents reveal the earlier locations of federal, state, and county highways, thus providing today's visitors with opportunities to see firsthand some examples of the older local culture.

Even if some people are unable to go home again, most of those who have ties with the Upper Cumberland have a deep and abiding sense of place. They treasure both their tangible and emotional ties with hearth and home and often long to return. Children sometimes accompany parents and grandparents who are attempting to retrace their steps along old paths once taken to church and school, while sharing stories of times that now exist only in their memories. Most of these sentimental journeys are thwarted, however, as flood control reservoirs, corporate farming enterprises, timber-cutting crews, bulldozers, and shopping centers continue to alter the landscape.

While the physical scene has changed in the Kentucky-Tennessee Upper Cumberland, cultural landmarks are still visible in this portion of the Upper South. As the twentieth century draws to a close, the Upper Cumberland of the nineteenth century endures in some important regards. Vestiges of beliefs and practices based on folk medicine are still in evidence, as are certain religious customs that hark back to the old ways of life and thought; a few farmers continue to work the land with horse-drawn implements; some craftspeople make their livings using methods and materials learned about from ancestors; and old-time musicians can be found who employ the same tunes and techniques as their pioneer forbears.

Equally important in maintaining continuity are such folklife forms as family foodways that, while not unique to the Upper Cumberland, remain so unchanged as to be virtually sacred; oral family narratives that inform present generations about earlier ones; and various forms of social activities that continue to link individuals, families, and communities.

Community schools and churches, along with the family, were the region's chief unifying agents through the first half of the twentieth century. These institutions operated along formal and informal lines to achieve social stability and change. Schools and churches especially separated males and females, thus reinforcing gender roles. Community schools no longer exist, and poorly attended rural churches play rather insignificant roles in the religious and social lives of Upper Cumberland residents. However, the family as an institution has maintained its prominence. Children continue to visit parents regularly, and the parents, sometimes in company with their children, participate in a wide range of convivial activities that take place in churches, schools, and community centers.

Most folk activities in the region are, on the surface, different from what they were years ago. However, the new forms are often rooted in the old, being the same kinds of activities with different faces. Old-time music sessions and play-parties have given way to newer forms of music and courtship games, but the same social requirements are met. Folk tradition seldom dies out; it only changes a bit in order to serve better the needs of a new generation. It seems likely that the Upper Cumberland will continue its leadership role in nurturing folklife forms and activities through countless years ahead.

Bibliographic Notes

INTRODUCTION

Any number of publications describe American regionalism and regional conscious-ness. Two excellent recent works include Barbara Allen and Thomas J. Schlereth, eds., *Sense of Place: American Regional Cultures* (Lexington: University Press of Kentucky, 1990), and Glen Lich, ed., *Regional Studies: The Interplay of Land and People* (College Station: Texas A & M University Press, 1992). A useful early compilation of essays on regionalism is Merrill Jensen, ed., *Regionalism in America* (Madison: University of Wisconsin Press, 1951), containing Lewis Wirth's "The Limitations of Regionalism," cited in the present study. Richard M. Dorson defines the term "folk region" in his *American Folklore* (Chicago: University of Chicago Press, 1958), p. 75. Willis B. Boyd, *The Upper Cumberlands* (Cookeville, TN 1939) provides descriptions of that region and insights into its economic plight and plans for recovery following the Great Depression.

Don Yoder includes working definitions of folklife in "The Folklife Studies Movement," *Pennsylvania Folklife* 13:3 (1963):43-56, and in Yoder, ed., *American Folklife* (Austin: University of Texas Press, 1976).

CHAPTER I

Valuable accounts of prehistoric life in Tennessee's Upper Cumberland include John Haywood's *The Natural and Aboriginal History of Tennessee up to the First Settlement . . .* (Nashville, 1823; rpt. Jackson, Tenn.: McCowat-Mercer Press, 1959); Charles Hudson, *The Southeastern Indians* (Knoxville: University of Tennessee Press, 1976); and Ronald N. Satz, *Tennessee's Indian Peoples* (Knoxville: University of Tennessee Press, 1979). Other works of interest include Harriette S. Arnow's *Seedtime on the Cumberland* (New York: Macmillan, 1960; rpt. Lexington, 1983), George E. Webb's "Peaceful Natives: Indians in the Upper Cumberland," in *Lend An Ear: Heritage of the Tennessee Upper Cumberland*, Calvin Dickinson et al., eds. (Lanham, New York, London: University Press of America, 1983), and Opless Walker, "Trails Worn Centuries Ago Have Left Imprints on Today's Landscape," Cookeville *Herald-Citizen*, May 12, 1991, 8–10.

There are no general history surveys of the Upper Cumberland region. However, my own *Don't Go Up Kettle Creek: Verbal Legacy of the Upper Cumberland* (Knoxville: University of Tennessee Press, 1983) contains much historical background information that complements the oral traditional narratives told by area residents about the region's history. Harriette S. Arnow's *Seedtime on the Cumberland* (1960) and *Flowering of the Cumberland* (New York: Macmillan, 1963; rpt. Lexington, 1984) are thoroughly researched accounts of the history and life along the Cumberland River, especially

Wayne County, Kentucky, and the Cumberland settlements in the Nashville Basin. Also of value is Alvin B. Wirt's *The Upper Cumberland of Pioneer Times* (Washington: privately published, 1954).

Numerous county and community histories have been published by private means. Some of these are well-written and contain much valuable information; others do little more than list the names of prominent families, individuals, and political office holders. The ones I found useful in preparing this chapter include Albert R. Hogue, *History of Fentress County, Tennessee* (Baltimore: Regional Publishing Co., 1975); George A. Knight, *My Album of Memories* (Knoxville: Southeastern Composition Services, 1971) and *Our Wonderful Overton County Heritage* (Knoxville: Southeastern Composition Services, 1972); Ernest M. Lawson, *Awakening of Cumberland County [Kentucky]* ... (Burkesville: Cumberland County Printing Co., 1973); William L. Montell, *Monroe County History, 1820–1970* (Tompkinsville: Monroe County Press, 1970); Monroe Seals, *History of White County* (Sparta: privately published, 1935); Molden J. Tayse, *Jackson County, Tennessee* (Gainesboro: privately published, 1989); and Garnet Walker, *Exploring Wayne County* (Monticello: privately published, 1966).

The history of African Americans in the Upper Cumberland has not been written. The only book-length study available so far is my own *The Saga of Coe Ridge: A Study in Oral History* (Knoxville: University of Tennessee Press, 1970), which deals exclusively with one settlement of black people in southern Cumberland County, Kentucky. Efforts to do research for that volume and for the present one point up the crucial need for a study devoted exclusively to the black population in the Upper Cumberland. Patricia Bell Scott's "Black Folklore in Tennessee: A Working Bibliography," *Tennessee Folklore Society Bulletin* 44 (1978): 130–33, affords a good starting point. Also helpful is Elizabeth Peterson and Tom Rankin's "Free Hill: An Introduction," *TSFB* 51 (Spring 1985): 1–7, a descriptive essay dealing with the historic black community near Celina. Peterson's "Trickster and Trader: Portrait of An Afro-American Entrepreneur" (Ph. D. diss., Indiana University, 1990) provides valuable insights into the life of Robert "Bud" Garrett, resident of Free Hill.

The beginnings of a new social and economic era for southern mountain people in general are described by Mary French Caldwell in "Change Comes to the Appalachian Mountaineer," *Current History,* 31 (February 1930): 961–67. For a look at the coming of modern times to the Upper Cumberland, consult the final chapter of Montell, *Don't Go Up Kettle Creek.* Also helpful in this regard are census records and other data available at the Lake Cumberland Area Development District Office in Russell Springs, Kentucky, and the Upper Cumberland Development District, Cookeville, Tennessee.

CHAPTER 2

Early architectural forms and construction technology are outlined in Michael Ann Williams, "Folk Architecture," *The Kentucky Encyclopedia*, John Kleber et al., eds. (Lexington: University Press of Kentucky, 1992), 338–39. For fuller descriptions and commentary on vernacular forms, consult William Lynwood Montell and Michael L. Morse, *Kentucky Folk Architecture* (Lexington: University of Kentucky Press, 1976).

Calvin Dickinson, "Our Fathers' Houses . . . ," in *Lend An Ear . . .*, Dickinson et al., eds., 77–88, affords a brief look at some of the more classical architectural forms in the region.

Researchers interested in early home life, living standards, religious life, and moral standards, are referred to J. C. Wright's edition of his father's monumentally important diary, issued under the title *Autobiography of Reverend Absalom B. Wright of the Holston Conference, M. E. Church* (Cincinnati: Cranston and Curts, 1896). Home life, home furnishings, and early forms of transportation are also described in detail by Joseph W. Wells, *History of Cumberland County [Ky.]* (Louisville: Standard Printing Co., 1947). Other helpful local histories include the Reverend C. L. Holt, *Seventy Years in the Cumberlands* (privately published, n.d.), 25; Monroe Seals, *History of White County* (1935), 12, 14, 92–93, 105, 145; Lynnie White, *Lest We Forget* (Monticello: privately published, 1974), 8–9, 30–31. Of some help are the various reports written during the 1930s by members of the Federal Writers Project of the Works Progress Administration. These documents, generally available for each county, are housed at the state libraries in Frankfort and Nashville.

Some attention to area housing and living conditions was given by Walter B. Overton, "An Educational, Economic, and Community Survey of Jackson County, Tennessee" (Master's thesis, University of Tennessee, 1927), 39–42. See also Margaret B. Des Champs, "Pioneer Life in the Cumberland Country" (Master's thesis, Vanderbilt University, 1946), and Arnow, *Seedtime . . .*, op, cit., 259 ff.

Two known published accounts of waterwitching in the Upper Cumberland are Lewis D. Bandy, "Witchcraft and Divination in Macon County," *Tennessee Folklore Society Bulletin*, 9 (May 1943): 1–13, and E. G. Rogers, "Switching for Water," *TFSB*, 21 (1955): 108–11. Interesting oral information about the witching process was shared by Quinn Davidson, a Pickett County dowser.

Ron Eller provides helpful comments about bartering as a way of life in "Land and Family: An Historical View of Preindustrial Appalachia," *Appalachian Journal*, (Winter, 1979): 83–110, esp. 95.

For folklife scholars, the task of defining folk art generally involves refuting prior definitions by art historians, art critics, and art collectors, who view folk art largely on the basis of aesthetics. Little attention is paid to the individual artists/craftspersons, the community in which the art was created, or the traditional nature of the art form. Folklorist Ann Taft writes in "The Evolving View of Folk Art," *Western Kentucky University Student Honors Research Bulletin* (1985–86), that folklorists now view folk art in terms of its artistic tradition, the artists, and the cultural environment in which the art was produced.

Essays on folk arts and crafts are quite numerous. Especially helpful in providing an overview of the topic in this chapter is Roby Cogswell's eight-page treatise, "History and Handcrafts in the Upper Cumberland Region"(unpublished ms., 1991). Equally important essays include Michael Ann Williams, "Folk Arts and Crafts," in *The Kentucky Encyclopedia*, op. cit., 333–34, and Sally Crain's "Handmade in Tennessee: Arts and Crafts in the Upper Cumberland," in *Lend An Ear . . .*, Dickinson et al., eds., 89–93. Chairmaking, basketry, and a host of other craft items, along with their makers in the Upper Cumberland, are described by Helen Bullard in *Crafts and Craftspeople of the Tennessee Mountains* (Falls Church, Va.: The Summit Press, Ltd., 1976). She earlier provided a valuable account of the Tabors, a chairmaking family in Cumberland County, Tennessee, in "Tabor Family Noted As Stout Chair Makers Over 150 Years," *The Tennessee Conservationist*, 22 (July 1956): 14–15. Chairmaking and furniture production by local craftspersons is dealt with in Lewis D. Bandy, "Folklore in Macon County, Tennessee" (Master's thesis, Peabody College, 1940).

A helpful essay on quilting is Sandra K. D. Stahl's "Quilts and A Quiltmaker's Aesthetics," *Indiana Folklore*, 11:2 (1978): 105–32. Excellent book-length accounts of quilting include Beth Ramsey and Merikay Waldvogel, *The Quilts of Tennessee: Images of Domestic Life Prior to 1930* (Nashville: Rutledge Hill Press, 1986) and Merikay Waldvogel, *Soft Covers for Hard Times: Quiltmaking and the Great Depression* (Nashville: Rutledge Hill Press, 1990). Specific attention to coverlets is provided by Sadye T. Wilson and Doris F. Kennedy, *Of Coverlets: The Legacies, The Weavers* (Nashville: Tunstede, 1983).

CHAPTER 3

Gender and age roles within family circles are described, however briefly, by Ina Ruth Grimsley, "Memories I Hold Dear," *Celina Globe*, August 31, 1969, 3; George A. Knight, *History of the Pioneers of Overton County* (Knoxville: Southeastern Composition Services, 1972), 148–50; Walter B. Overton (Master's thesis, op. cit.), 41; Lynnie White, *Lest We Forget*, op cit., 6–7. Oral recollections were provided by Ova Allred, Crawford, Overton County, June 18, 1976; Landon Anderson, Celina, and Albert Bilbrey, Gainesboro, March 12, 1976; Cora and Sherman Burnett, Sunnybrook, Wayne County, September 14, 1983; Gladys Stone, Celina, interviewed by Becky Morse April 16, 1976.

Bruce McWhorter's "Superstitions from Russell County, Kentucky," *Kentucky Folklore Record* (January–March 1966): 11–14, contains beliefs pertaining to pregnancy, birthing, and caring for the baby.

Nonfolkloric studies recommended for general and scholarly reading include Patricia D. Beaver, *Rural Community in the Appalachian South* (Lexington: University Press of Kentucky, 1986); F. Carlene Bryant, *We're All Kin* (Knoxville: University of Tennessee Press, 1981); John Demos, *Past, Present and Personal* (New York: Oxford University Press, 1986); Margaret J. Hagood, *Mothers of the South* (1939; rpt. New York: W. W. Norton and Company, 1977); Elmora M. Matthews, *Neighbor and Kin* (Nashville: Vanderbilt University Press, 1966); and entries by Orville V. Burton, Thomas D. Clark, Catherine Clinton, Sharon Sharp, Steven M. Stowe, Charles Wilson, and Margaret Wolfe in *The Encyclopedia of Southern Culture*, Charles Wilson and William Ferris, eds. (Jackson: The University Press of Mississippi, 1989).

Publications on folk toys and playthings are plentiful, but serious scholarly studies are scarce. Worthy of mention here are Elinor L. Horwitz, *Mountain People, Mountain Crafts* (Philadelphia: J. B. Lippincott, 1974), which contains a section on dolls and toys; and Dick Schnacke, *American Folk Toys . . . and How To Make Them* (New York: G. P. Putnam's Sons, 1973), a book that was developed from information collected by Richard Chase and his chauffeur. Allen H. Eaton, *Handicrafts of the Southern Highlands* (New York: Russell Sage Foundation, 1937), has a chapter on toy making and includes numerous photographs of handmade toys.

The July 1980 issue of *Western Folklore* is devoted exclusively to children's folklore. A comprehensive bibliography and collection of scholarly essays on the subject is contained in *Issues in Children's Folklore*, edited by Brian Sutton-Smith, Jay Mechling, and Thomas W. Johnson (Washington: Smithsonian Institution Press, 1988). For a sampling of children's folklore, consult Simon J. Bronner, ed., *American Children's Folklore* (Little Rock: August House, 1988). Local publications containing descriptions of children's toys and playthings include Lynnie White, *Lest We Forget*, 5–6; Peggy B. Boaz, "Take It Off, Knock It Off, Or Let the Crows Pick It Off," *Tennessee Folklore Society Bulletin*, 39 (1973): 77–78, and Robert Lassiter, "Games We Played," *TFSB*, 12:1 (1946) 17–22. Oral accounts of childhood play and other forms of recreation were provided by Hiram Parrish, Burkesville (1975); Carlos Pitcock, Meshack, Monroe County (interviewed by Sue Ann Thompson, August 5, 1981); Katherine and Sam Anderson, Gainesboro, June 4, 1991.

Children's games have long captivated the attention of folklife scholars. Peter and Ionie Opie published at least five books on these and related activities of children between 1947 and 1973, including *Children's Games in Street and Playground* (Oxford: Clarendon Press, 1969).

Courtship and courtship games of young adults are described by Lewis D. Bandy, "Folklore in Macon County, Tennessee" (Master's thesis, op, cit.), 12–13, 30–32, 139–50; Patricia G. Lane, "Birth, Marriage, and Death: Past and Present Customs in East Tennessee," *TFSB* 48 (Summer 1982): 53–59; Harry Law, "Some Folklore of Macon County," *TFSB*, 18 (December 1952): 97–100; L. L. McDowell, "A Background of Folklore," *TFSB*, 2 (January 1936): 1–8; *Monroe County Folklife*, ed. Lynwood Montell (Tompkinsville: Monroe County Press, 1975), 59–78; 4–5; Lynnie White, *Lest We Forget*, 50–51. Of interest here also is Marion H. Skean's *Circle Left: Folk-Play of the Kentucky Mountains* (Ary, Ky.: Homeplace, 1939), 1–48. Oral descriptions were provided by Ward Curtis, Strodetown, Monroe County (September 23, 1983); Roy Deckard, Tompkinsville (interviewed by Sharen and Karen Walden, December, 1974); Bethel Holloway, Calfkiller Valley, Putnam County, interviewed by Brad Simpson, David Storie and Anne Zachari, November 9, 1979); and Adele Mitchell, Edmonton, Metcalfe County (interviewed by Carolyn Best, February 1, 1976).

Regional treatments of the play-party include Lewis D. Bandy, "Folklore in Macon County," op. cit., 143–44; L. L. McDowell, "Finding Folk Dances in Tennessee," *TFSB*, 4 (Winter 1938): 90–99; Ruth W. O'Dell, "Tennessee Play-Parties," *TFSB*, 18 (Fall 1952): 68–71. Oral descriptions of the play-party were provided by Jim Bowles, Darlene Carter and Elsworth Carter, Rock Bridge, Monroe County (1958); Daily Crouch and Edd Moody, Moodyville, Pickett County (1976); Lynnie White, Monticello (interviewed by Nancy Daffron, September 17, 1976).

Published accounts of shivarees relevant here include those by such local writers as Bandy, "Folklore of Macon County," op. cit., 28–30; Patricia G. Lane, "Birth, Marriage, and Death...," 55; Molden Tayse, *Jackson County* (1989), 79; and Mel Tharp, "Shivaree," *Kentucky Folklore Record*, 22 (October–December, 1976): 102–103. Various oral sources are cited in *Monroe County Folklife*, ed. Lynwood Montell (1975), 72–73.

CHAPTER 4

National patterns in education and educational reforms are described in numerous books and articles. Of special significance is historian David Tyack's *The One Best System: A History of American Urban Education* (Cambridge: Harvard University Press, 1974). Of immediate relevance to the present description of academies, subscription schools, and free public schools in the Upper Cumberland are Harriette S. Arnow,

Flowering of the Cumberland (New York: Macmillan, 1963; rpt. Lexington: University Press of Kentucky, 1984). 156–92; Ira Bell, *History of Public Education of Wayne County, 1842–1975* (Monticello: Lakeview Printing, Inc., 1976); the Reverend C. L. Holt, *Seventy Years in the Cumberlands* (n.p., n.d.), passim; George A. Knight, *Our Wonderful Overton* (Knoxville: Southeastern Composition Services, 1972), 79–93; Lynwood Montell, ed., *Monroe County Folklife* (Tompkinsville: Monroe County Press, 1975), 64–76; Pickett County Historical Committee, *History and Genealogy of Families in Pickett County* (Byrdstown: Privately published, 1991), 138–85; Monroe Seals, *History of White County* (Sparta: 1935), 33–39; Judge Joseph W. Wells, *This or That* (Louisville: Standard Printing Company, 1966), 21–22; and Lynnie White, *Lest We Forget,* op. cit., 1974), 17–20. Gordon Wilson's four-part article on one-room schools in western Kentucky published in *Kentucky Folklore Record,* 13: 1–4 (1967), provides an invaluable source of information and ideas, as does Walter B. Overton's *Educational, Economic, and Community Survey of Jackson County, Tennessee,* op. cit., passim. Bandy's 1940 Master's thesis, op. cit., contains several descriptions of school play-time activities in and around Lafayette.

Equally important were the oral accounts about one-room schools and related play-time activities provided between 1976 and 1981 by Landon Anderson of Clay County; Hiram Parrish and Arnold Watson of Cumberland County, Kentucky; Albert Bilbrey, Mary Cummings, Claude Hackett, and Lena Howell Martin, all of Jackson County; Ruth VanZant (interviewed by Carolyn Best) of Metcalfe County; my own personal recollections of the one-room schools at Rock Bridge and Merryville in Monroe County; George Allred (black), native of Overton County and later resident of Monroe County; Morris Gaskin of Russell County; Ira Bell and Garnet Walker of Wayne County.

In general, today's religious beliefs and expression in the Upper Cumberland derive from a rich and dynamic pioneer tradition. The Great Revival, which began in Kentucky around 1800 and traveled to Tennessee, served as a catalyst to establish many current beliefs and customs. For an intriguing account of the spiritual and economic conditions contributing to the Great Revival, see John Boles, *The Great Revival* (Lexington: University of Kentucky Press, 1972). Of particular interest because of their references to camp meetings are William G. West's *Barton W. Stone: Early American Advocate for Christian Unity* (Nashville: Disciples of Christ Historical Society, 1954) and *The Autobiography of Peter Cartwright: The Backwoods Preacher* (New York: Charlton and Porter, 1857).

Herbert Asbury eulogized Francis Asbury in *A Methodist Saint: The Life of Bishop Asbury* (New York: Alfred A. Knopf, 1927), a volume that is valuable for its remarks concerning the circuit-riding system and the bishop's journal. The careers of Raccoon John Smith and Reverend Billy Cooper are summarized in Augusta P. Johnson's *A Century of Wayne County, Kentucky, 1800–1900* (Louisville: Standard Printing Co., 1939). Roy West's "Pioneer Preachers: Religion in the Upper Cumberland," appears in Calvin Dickinson, et. al, eds. *Lend An Ear: Heritage of the Tennessee Upper Cumberland* (Lanham, Md.: University Press of America, 1983), 21–32. Beatrice Powell provides an enjoyable and informative essay, "The Old Fashioned Association," *Kentucky Folklore Record,* 6:3 (July–September, 1960): 77–85. Timothy Cantrell, "A History of Baptists in Clinton County, Kentucky" (Master's thesis, Western Kentucky University, 1969), cites Viebie Cantrell's unpublished manuscript titled "All Day Meeting and Dinner on the Ground," a 1968 document that describes the associational gatherings and points out the diminished sense of neighborliness resulting from their demise. Mel Tharp's article, "When the Preacher Came to Visit," *Tennessee Folklore Society Bulletin,* 43:3 (June 1977): 135–37, provides a humor-filled look at home life when a visiting minister is present. Folklorist Homer Kemp looks at preaching in the Upper Cumberland both seriously and humorously in his feature story, "Somewhar Betwixt the Lids of the Goodbook," *Standing Stone Press*, Monterey, Tenn. (Summer, 1982), 3.

Oral interviews that produced valuable comments about old-time religion include those conducted in the late 1970s with George Allred (Monroe County), Albert Bilbrey and Lena Howell Martin (Jackson County), Coyle Copeland (Overton County), Hazel Montell (Monroe County), and the Reverend Gifford Walters (Wayne County).

CHAPTER 5

For a general approach to the study of recent trends and analyses in natural and magico-religious medical practices, consult *American Folk Medicine: A Symposium*, Wayland D. Hand, ed. (Berkeley: University of California Press, 1976), which contains essays delivered by academicians and members of the scientific medical community alike. A contributor to that volume was David J. Hufford of the Hershey Medical School, who also wrote "Customary Observances in Modern Medicine," *Western Folklore* 48 (APRIL 1989): 129–43.

Publications from the Upper Cumberland containing information on some facet of folk medical practices include Bandy, "Macon County," op. cit., 167–70; Floyd B. Hay, *The Country Doctor* (Albany: privately published, 1983); Harry Law, "Some Folklore of Macon County," *Tennessee Folklore Society Bulletin*, 18 (December 1952): 97–100; Montell, *Monroe County Folklife*, 90–93; Ruby R. Norris, "Folk Medicine of Cumberland County," *Kentucky Folklore Record*, 4 (July–September 1958): 101–10; Seals, *History of White County*, 16–17; J. W. Wells, *This or That* (Louisville: Standard Printing Co., 1966), 12–13; Mary C. Wharton, *Doctor Woman of the Cumberlands* (Pleasant Hill, Tenn.: Uplands Press, 1953). Richard M. Raichelson's "Belief and Effectivity: Folk Medicine in Tennessee," *Tennessee Folklore Society Bulletin*, 49 (Fall 1983): 103–106, is also relevant here.

Writings about area mineral resorts include Bandy, op. cit., 20–23; "Bloomington Springs Has Illustrious Past," *The Gainesboro Times*, January 28, 1972, 1; "Donoho Hotel: A Quiet Visit Into the Past," *The Jackson County Times*, July 12, 1974, 7; "Famed Springs Result in Formation of Russell Springs, Ky. in 1899," *The Times Journal*, Jamestown, July 4, 1974, 8–9; "Rebirth of Red Boiling Springs Well Underway," *The Celina Globe*, May 18, 1961, 1; "Red Boiling Springs: Nature's Clinic for Sick People," *Jackson County Times*, May 7, 1975, 18; Seals, *White County*, 51–52, 65; "Happy Clang of the Dinner Bell [at the Donoho Hotel]," in Hugh Walker, *Tennessee Tales* (Nashville: Aurora Press, 1970), 69–70.

In addition to the persons identified in the chapter narrative, others who contributed oral testimonials about folk medicine and its local practitioners include Albert Bilbrey, Whitleyville, Jackson County; Sherman and Cora Burnett, Sunnybrook, Wayne County; Coyle Copeland, Crawford, Overton County; Emma Crabtree (black), Gainesboro; Bob Dudney, Gainesboro; Bertha Mae Key, Hanging Limb, Overton County; Lena Howell Martin, Gainesboro, Edd Moody, Moodyville, Pickett County; Nell C. Taylor, Byrdstown; Edith Williams, Celina.

Several articles in folklore journals were helpful in developing ideas for the section on death and burial. These include Jimmy D. Browning, "A Tie That Binds: Contemporary Funeral Foodways in Rural Kentucky," *Tennessee Folklore Society Bulletin,* 55:1 (Spring 1991): 14–25; Wayne Geurin, "Some Folkways of A Stuart County Community," *Tennessee Folklore Society Bulletin,* 19 (September 1953): 49–52; Patricia G. Lane, "Birth, Marriage, and Death: Past and Present Customs in East Tennessee," *Tennessee Folklore Society Bulletin,* 50 (Summer 1984): 58–66, esp. 64–66; Marilyn Whitley, "The Burial of the Dead: Customs, Beliefs, and Superstitions from Franklin County, North Carolina," *North Carolina Folklore,* 25 (Summer 1977): 61–66.

The various forms of gravehouses are described by Brent Cantrell, "Traditional Grave Structures on the Eastern Highland Rim," *Tennessee Folklore Society Bulletin,* 47 (Fall 1981): 93–103; Lynwood Montell, "Cemetery Decoration Customs in the American South," in Robert E. Walls and George H. Shoemaker, eds., *The Old Traditional Way of Life* (Bloomington: Trickster Press, 1989), 111–29; and Anita Pitchford, "The Material Culture of the Traditional East Texas Graveyard," *Southern Folklore Quarterly,* 43 (1979): 277–90.

Invaluable also were oral interviews with Harold Beard, Adair County (conducted by Donna Morrison in 1965); James Franklin Butler, Cumberland County, Ky., February 27, 1976; Henry Guffey, Wayne County (conducted by Betty Dalton in 1965); Richard Lee, funeral director, Monticello (conducted by Marjorie Bow, 1976); Lena Howell Martin, Gainesboro, 1976; Dr. and Mrs. Owsley, Burkesville; Ruth Van Zant, Edmonton (conducted by Carolyn Best, February 8, 1976); Arnold Watson, Cumberland County, Ky., January 9, 1976; Clyde "Bully" White, Monroe County (conducted by Karen and Sharen Walden, December, 1973).

CHAPTER 6

Little fieldwork has been done on social stratification among teenagers and the terms used to describe the phenomenon. Neither is there much available information on cruising, hanging out, and the car culture in general.

The relationship between youth and the automobile has been examined to some extent by sociologists. A. B. Hollingshead's *Elmtown's Youth* (New York: Wiley and Sons, 1949) provides keen insight into the perpetuation of class stratification in youth culture and looks as well at the town's disdain for delinquent uses of the automobile. The reader should also be aware of Robert S. Lynd and Helen M. Lynd, *Middletown* (New York: Harcourt, Brace and Co., 1929), a book that describes the automobile as a threat to the traditions associated with home and religion, and their *Middletown Revisited: A Study in Cultural Conflicts* (1937). Finally, Michael L. Berger's *The Devil Wagon in God's Country: The Automobile and Social Change in Rural America, 1893–1929* (Hamden, Conn: Archon Books, 1979) provides an excellent multidisciplinary look at the automobile's effects on such cultural matters as leisure, religion, education, health, and environment.

Folkloric descriptions of these activities include James P. Leary's "Hanging Out: Recreational Folklore in Everyday Life" in *Handbook of American Folklore,* Richard M. Dorson, ed. (Chicago: University of Chicago Press, 1983) 178–82. Worthy of mention here also is Richard Reuss's "Suburban Folklore," also found in Dorson's

Handbook of American Folklore, 172–177, and Michael Licht's "Some Automotive Play Activities of Suburban Teenagers," *New York Folklore Quarterly*, 30 (1974): 44–65.

For an excellent interpretive description of the slumber party, consult Julia Woodbridge Oxrieder, "The Slumber Party: Transition into Adolescence," *Tennessee Folklore Society Bulletin* 43 (Fall, 1977): 128–34. The twenty essays by Teresa Scott's students at Clinton County Elementary School were contributed by Misty Bowlin, Stephanie Claborn, Katresa Collins, Tonya Conatser, Sarah Dalton, Tabitha Davis, Adam Denney, Sabrina Dicken, Lucas Fazzary, Joni Hicks, Bethany Little, Adam Marcum, Samantha Marcum, Amanda Parrigin, Shannon Perdue, Beverly Phillips, Brent Riddle, Crystal Smith, Nick Upchurch, and Misty Winningham. A hearty and sincere "thank you" to all of them.

Students and others who provided personal comments and descriptions about stratification, cruising, and hanging out include, from Albany (Clinton County), Brandy Baker, Joey Craig, Jr., Jeremy Derryberry, Shelby Jean Frost Flowers, and Shawn Heist; from Burkesville (Cumberland County), Michael Brandon, Keith Cash, Sarah Scott, and Libby Smith; from Cookeville (Putnam County), Scotty Garrett, Shane Roberts and Jesse Webber; from Edmonton (Metcalfe County), Jeremy Harrison, Randy Meyers, Ginger and Selena Nunn, and Mike Raney; from Jamestown/Russell Springs (Russell County), Damion Anderson, Davene Clark, John Dillon, Ronnie Draper, Kristi Feece, Billy Grider, Monica Jenkins, John McNay, Torrie Naeyaert, Keith Scholl, Laura Sharp, Sara Sheats, and Kim Withers; from Jamestown, Tennessee (Fentress County), one unidentified male 1990 high school graduate; from Lafayette (Macon County), Michelle Brown, Tonya Capps, Joy Carr, Stacy Carver, Chris Peterson, April Stone, and Michael Underwood; from Livingston (Overton County), Jim Bowman, Marilyn Breeding, Martin Evans, Brenda Moon, and three unidentified recent female graduates of Livingston High who were check-out girls at a local super market; from Sparta (White County), Robert Gibbs (black) and John Robinson (black).

CHAPTER 7

The four loafers at Whitleyville, Jackson County, were Steve Cassetty, Wesley Cassetty, Billy Dawes, and Dale Mercer.

Numerous feature stories about rolly hole marbles have appeared in Louisville, Nashville, Cookeville, and other area newspapers. Otherwise, this fascinating regional game has been described in a scholarly context by only one folklorist, Becky Morse. Her brief article, "Rolly Hole: A Regional Marble Game," appeared in the *Kentucky Folklore Record* (April–June 1977): 41–44. Bobby Fulcher, folklorist with the Tennessee Department of Parks and Recreation, annually issues a pamphlet describing the rolly hole game for persons in attendance at the annual Standing Stone State Park event.

A brief note by James T. Stewart on "Recollections of Life in Western Hart During the Early 1900s," *Hart County Historical Society Quarterly*, 21:4 (October 1989): 8–9, states that a "three-hole marble" game was once known in that Kentucky county, located about twenty miles northwest of the study area. Sam Anderson, native of Warren County, Tennessee, claims that he knew of rolly hole marble games there in the 1920s and 1930s.

Oral sources on rolly hole marbles include John Boles, Travis Cherry, Bud Garrett, James Lane, and Dumas Walker, all of whom were interviewed by Bobby Fulcher in 1983. I personally interviewed George Carter, Dumas Walker, and Welby Lee in the mid-1970s.

Of help in connection with understanding hunter culture were Francis E. Abernathy, "The East Texas Communal Hunt," in *Hunters and Healers: Folklore Types and Topics*, Wilson M. Hudson, ed. (Austin: The Encino Press, 1971), 3–10, and Fred Kniffen, "Notes and Queries," *Journal of American Folklore*, 62 (1949): 187–88. Of the numerous popular press items available, I drew upon only H. Lea Lawrence, "Of Boars 'n' Bows," *Bowhunter* (January 1989): 20–22.

Rebecca Hornal of Bowling Green provided considerable input about female bonding agents and assisted me in writing about women hunters in the Upper Cumberland.

Helpful accounts of cockfighting include James E. Cobb, "Cockfighting in East Tennessee," *Glimpses of Southern Appalachian Folk Culture: Papers in Memory of Norbert F. Riedl*, Charles H. Faulkner and Carol K. Buckles, eds. (Knoxville: Tennessee Anthropological Association, 1978), 75–96, and Steven L. Del Sesto, "Roles, Rules, and Organization...of Cockfighting in Rural Louisiana," *Southern Folklore Quarterly*, 39 (March 1975): 1–14.